K.A. Perkins

**Published by: G & P Unlimited Co. L.L.C.
K. A. Perkins
Dayton, Ohio 45406
ISBN: 978-1-7369074-0-5
Copyright 2021 by K.A. Perkins
All rights reserved.**

In whole or in part without the author's written consent, the Reproduction of the text is not permitted and unlawful according to the 1976 United States Copyright Act. Printed and distributed by G&P Unlimited Co. LLC.

G & P UNLTD. CO. INTERACTIVE

At G & P Unlimited Co., we are excited to offer our branded series of Interactive books. Interactive books are used to help you, the reader, to organize and learn the information covered in this book. The reasoning behind creating interactive books originated with actual research-based classroom instructional strategies like notetaking, concept mapping, and organizing information to assist your learning. G&P Unlimited Interactive books' goal combines all this research into one instructional method to promote your education. We do this through charts, infographics, visualizations, and journaling.

We purposefully designed this book to be larger so that you can use the margins and open spaces to draw, doodle, and document inspired thought. So, write in the book, color, and draw. Make this book your learning masterpiece; what you will discover is that as you engage with this book, it will empower your life. Remember to carry your pencils!

Share your masterpiece! We are creators just like you, and we would love to see your interpretation of what you have learned and your engagement with this interactive book. Please email us at info@gpunltd.com or use hashtag #**GPINTERACTIVE.**

Forward-Hustle Mentality

Your life is forged with a purpose that was designed at the time you were conceived. That purpose is not only spiritual but is universal; your existence impacts the lives of others. Your contribution to humanity is important and it is the real reason that you are holding this book. Years ago, I made it my mission to Hustle to the point I would die empty; to leave a legacy of fulfilled dreams on the battlefield of life. It with that heart that I wrote this book. The skill, competencies, and principles covered in this manual are tools designed to help your Hustle. Everything in this manual is intended to be your strength in times of weakness and to be your light when you want to give up.

Over the years, I have learned that it is impossible to fulfill destiny and purpose if you are chasing money. Your vision for your life must be transcendent. While money is important real success is organic and can never be achieved through materialism.

Money is lovely; but does your Hustle make you happy? Hustle Culture is the balance achieved when you make money by doing that which makes you happy. The decision to have a Hustle life is a decision of faith and hope. It is fighting the inward war that attempts to capture your authentic self, resulting in you living an inauthentic life. We all crave stability, but Hustle Culture requires faith courage to face fear in the pursuit of purpose.

Take me for example, I have always wanted to have my own business in public speaking. I inspired to speak to large groups of people, empowering them to be the best that they possibly could. However, in my 20's and 30's, I felt the need to have a stable income, to get a paycheck and insurance. I needed to be a responsible adult and take care of my responsibilities. I spent years working at being a responsible adult but neglecting my authentic self. Hence, my life was miserable. I was overworked, and unappreciated. When I decided to live my life based on purpose, things began to change. It was not an overnight process but choosing to be who I was created to be unlocked the Hustle Culture within. It took years to write this book! It took years of humbling situations, circumstances, and growth moments to publish a book that taught everything that people needed to know in order to escape the pits of life.

I know what it means to decide between inauthentic life and a life of purpose, vision, and mission; I know how it feels to need the security of a well-calculated plan for your future. The reality is that even if you attempt to ignore it, your purpose and vision for your life never changes.

You must decide if the grind is more important than living a life of the Hustle. The problem is that no day is promised. You may never know the outcome of your destiny if you never go for it. You only get one shot at living life, so you better master the art of living it!

Here my point: if you are reading this manual, that means that this manual is a part of your destiny and mine as well. My thoughts and my story are a part of your life. Whether you purchased this manual from me, ordered the book, received it as a gift, or found the book, it was all a part of a plan to help you achieve your purpose and to inspire you on your journey.

The reality is that if I had chosen a job over my passion, my purpose, vision, and mission, you would not be reading this book. It would be locked away in my mind and it would be mere information and thoughts rotting, until I decided to partner with destiny. Hustle Culture is monumental because it impacts your contribution to this world. For this reason, the destiny orchestrated that you find this book. Now you must choose to read it and make it apart of your life.

You cannot control time, but you can manage your choices as you leverage time. You can choose if you are going to partner with destiny. You can choose what you do with your time here on earth. You can choose whether you want to participate in a hustle culture. How you will be remembered will be how you have leveraged time, **Hustle Culture**.

Hustle Culture Contents

SECTION I: The Dilemma 8
    Eerie Silence 8
    Hustle Culture Manual 9
    Critical Need 12
    Teach Rules, Not Poverty 14
    This Manual Is for You 15

SECTION II: Leaving *Grind* to Find Hustle 18

SECTION III-Welcome Hustle Culture 25
    Hustle vs. *Grind* 29
    Niche Market Age 29
    Formula for Success 30
    Definition of Hustle 30
    Definition of *Grind* 32

SECTION IV: Hustle Culture Paradigm Shift 35
    The True Purpose of Education 44

SECTION V-Skills, Competencies, and Principals 51
    Pillar 1-Hustle Culture Skills 53
        1. Work Ethic 54
        2. Soft Skills 57
        3. Verbal Communication 86
        4. Written Communication 88
        5. Teamwork 89
        6. Leadership Skills 89
        7. Research Skills 91
        8. Assimilating Data 91
        9. Data Interpretation 92
    10. Problem Solving 92

Pillar 2-Hustle Culture Competencies 93
    1. Technological Competence 94
    2. Cultural Competence 96
    3. Global Competence 96
    4. Environmental Competence 97
    5. Political and Civic Competence 98

6. Industry/Corporate Competence 99
7. Financial Competence 99
8. Entrepreneurship Competence 101
9. Personal Branding Competence 103
10. Self Maintenance Competence 103

Pillar 3-Hustle Culture Principles 105

Principle One: Live and Release Your Pearls of Possibility 106
Principle Two: Hustlers Fellowship with Hustlers 107
Principle Three: Continue to Always Have Tikvah 108
Principle Four: Have a Spirit of Excellence-Give it Your All 108
Principle Five: Have Faith to Drown 109
Principle Six: Chill Out, Be Amazing, Be In-Control 112
Principle Seven: It Is Never Too Late 112
Principle Eight: Take Risk 113
Principle Nine: Everyday Must Count 114
Principle Ten: It is the LIL (Loyalty is Life) Thing 115
Principle Eleven: A Changed Mind is a Changed Life 116
Principle Twelve: Develop Productive Habits 116
Principle Thirteen: Collaboration 117
Principle Fourteen: Can't Stop, Won't Stop Mentality 118
Principle Fifteen: Find Your Fight 118
Principle Sixteen: Healthy Lifestyle 119
Principle Seventeen: Habits-The Making or Breaking Factor 119
Principle Eighteen: Do You and Be Epic About It 120
Principle Nineteen: Learn to Soar 121
Principle Twenty: Have a Clearly Defined Mission and Vision 122

SECTION VI: Hustle Transformation 138

Law One- The Law of Action Planning 138
Law Two-Law of Building 139
Law Three- Law of Being 140

Section VII-Conclusion 142

Section IX-Resources 144

SECTION I: The Dilemma

Eerie Silence

If you could ask an Executive of a Fortune 500 Company a series of questions, what would those questions be? What questions would you ask a person that is successfully living their dreams? These are the two questions that I asked a group of high school students five days before their graduation. These students did not voice any questions or utter a word! Based on their facial expressions, I saw that they understood the main point behind my question, specifically what they would need to ask in order to find the key to success; but their silence indicated that they did not know what to ask as it related to the specific tools that they lacked.

These young people were bright, hardworking, and resilient; however, when given the opportunity to ask questions that would provide insight, on how to create the future that they wanted, they did not know what to ask. One of the students who was utterly annoyed with my questions responded, "I know how to get money; I am gonna be good!" The student's response to what was intended to be an innocent question revealed a frustration that was deeply hidden within the shadows: they could visualize success, but they lacked the skills, competencies and principles needed to bring it to reality. My questions uncovered the shocking truth of economic disparity. There is a massive information gap when it comes to teaching personal and professional development strategies to teens and young adults, let alone poor, minority students. The student's lack of a response to my question did not take me by surprise. My questions uncovered the hard truth that we, as employers, educators, and parents, have failed to empower our young people. As adults, we haphazardly assume that schooling and exposure to individuals that have established some measure of success is enough to spark the fuel for their personal and professional development. Their eerie silence showed that we need to teach workforce rules to bridge the gap. This gap is exasperated when the students have to also overcome extreme poverty and trauma to secure employment after graduation.

Why would these students ask questions when they have been in survival mode their entire life? In essence, their quest to obtain their diploma is deep-rooted in their personal commitment and determination to create a better life for themselves. However, they were not equipped with the tools needed to better their life. These students were not afraid to ask questions, they purely lacked the essential knowledge to ask the right ones. The student's eerie silence and frustration prompted me to finish and publish Hustle Culture. In writing and publishing Hustle Culture, I found that this manual's content is a foundation of a movement. This manual is a crusade to give everyone, regardless of age or economic status, a solid footing to build a life of personal and professional success.

Hustle Culture Manual

Hustle Culture is a culmination of 20-years' worth of skills, competencies, and principles that I have learned, all documented in a manual formatted book. This manual is a collection of notes, instruments, and tools that I have used in coaching sessions, seminars, workshops, and classrooms. Hustle Culture is built on core workforce standards that never change. As you plan for your future, regardless of if you are pursuing additional schooling, entering the job market, or starting your own business, the workforce community is always evolving. You will soon find that every technological advancement, global and political initiative, economic development, and environmental innovation will impact the job market. The good thing is that regardless of these changes, Hustle Culture's core standards will never lose their relevance; they are applicable if you are just starting out or becoming a CEO of a major corporation.

See, when I graduated from high school, there were two things I believed:
1. **Drive was essential for success; and,**
2. **Regardless of their credentials, no one would ever out work me.**

Ever since high school and college, I have energetically researched and studied

everything I could that related to enhancing my skills, competencies, and principles in an effort to have a workforce advantage. I knew back then that my college degree was not going to prepare me for the world of work. I was convinced that having specific skills, competencies, and principles, coupled with ambition and drive, would give me an advantage in the job market. It was evident that I needed the know-how to leverage my weaknesses, to the point that my strengths opened remarkable doors of corporate opportunity. The blessing is that 20 years later, my research has allowed me to live an amazing life. I have impacted the lives of thousands, employed hundreds, and the Hustle keeps getting better every day.

I want to do the same for you! I want to share what I have learned along the way. I want to give you the tools needed to live the life of your dreams.

In my journey, I have observed many of my friends, family members, employees and co-workers become victims of their workforce shortcomings. Many of them lacked the necessary skills, principles, and competencies needed to succeed. I have watched many credentialed folks with natural talents fail to move up the corporate ladder. These individuals, though highly trained, where denied growth opportunities because they lacked the necessary tools outlined in this book. I realized twenty years ago that Hustle Culture was essential to anyone who needed help in personal and workforce development.

Helping people live better lives is my passion. What I have learned and applied in my career changed my life and I am committed to sharing that information with you. Twenty years ago, I started having conversations with everyone who would listen about the tools required to get promotions. Those conversations intensified and become more detail oriented. I started writing guides and coaching people to help them secure upper management positions. The results of these guides, discussions, sessions, and meetings laid the groundwork and became the roadmap for Hustle Culture. Everything covered in this book resulted from a lifetime of research, trial, and error.

There is nothing special about my journey; like most professionals, I have experienced numerous failures, disappointments, and growth-moments. I have had to rebuild my career. I have had to walk away from unhealthy work situations. I have experienced the setbacks of non-renewed contracts and termination. I even have been overlooked for promotion. The only difference between my journey and that of others is that I took the time to reflect on my failures, hone in on my research and make the necessary adjustments to my toolbox to make my Hustle stronger. Most importantly, I stopped caring about what people thought about me and took risks to grow as a person and as a professional.

I have found that the time-tested tools in Hustle Culture have always helped me land on my feet and quickly move up the corporate ladder. These Hustle Culture concepts are my foundation and reference point amid the constant demands to produce results under extreme pressure, tight deadlines, and minimal resources (money). Hustle Culture is a beacon of hope that inspires personal determination, hard work, and resiliency.

If you are struggling and need hope, Hustle Culture is for you. I know how important happiness is, and I understand the value of fulfilling one's dreams. Hustle Culture will teach you how to fulfill your destiny and purpose. Every topic, when mastered, is a key that will empower your life. Trust me, the Hustle Culture approach produces personal and professional success. As you read this manual, your life will shoot from the ordinary to the extraordinary. Whatever your fight is (poverty, terrible home life, racial or gender issues, or educational insufficiency) I promise that Hustle Culture will create lifelong success over time. I know because I am a product of what I am sharing with you.

Critical Need

Lastly, Hustle Culture meets a critical need in workforce culture and workforce development. Studies have shown that there is a significant workforce gap in America. Many corporations are incapable of hiring people with the skills and abilities needed to excel in their businesses. Corporations are also struggling to hire candidates that are equipped to work in even entry-level positions. While the data is frightening, this deficit signifies limitless opportunities to empower people to fill the current vacancies in the job market.

The numbers do not lie! At this very moment, you are holding tools that can change your life because the job market needs people like you! **The Strada-Gallup 2017 college scholar survey revealed that only one-third of college students (34 – 36%) believed that they graduated with the abilities and expertise to succeed in the competitive marketplace** (Gallup, 2017). Many of these same undergraduates revealed that their universities did not adequately prepare them to plunge into their careers. **The National Association of Colleges and Employers (NACE) found that only 42 % of employers felt newly hired employees met workplace standards** (Kelly, 2019). These same employers indicated that these recent graduates lacked problem-solving, collaboration, leadership, and career management.

Every person, regardless of socio-economic background, can now get into the workforce arena if they can get the job done. The power of Americas' workforce propels the American Dream. Since the data implies a universal gap in workforce ready college students, then it is valid to assume that working young adults from poverty communities are in a state of emergency. The national deficit means that a **Hustle Culture education can give anyone, regardless of who they are, an opportunity. This book is a battle plan that will allow you to compete against anyone.** What you have in your hand is the future of workforce development. If you take heed to what is in this manual, you will never be without work, and you will never live a life of poverty.

Let me explain why you will never be unemployed or poor again: Hustle Culture will give you a leverage and an advantage that most job seekers will lack. Every employer, potential client, and customer will expect that you possess the skills, principles, and competencies needed to perform a job. They assume that you have a mastery of the industry rules. Unfortunately, their assumptions are wrong because everyone does not know or have the skills, competencies, and principles needed to be efficient in their industry. This deficiency makes them victims of the job market instead of victors. The reality is that the victimization is not their fault; instead, the fault lies with schools, organizations, and enrichment programs that lack the curriculum that will expose their participants to problem-solving, teamwork, leadership, and career management. Hustle Culture gives you the strategic advantage by providing you with the curriculum they are missing.

The aim of Hustle Culture is to expose you, and anyone who wants to learn, to the unwritten rules that govern workforce culture. See, my business is in urban education; I know first-hand that these skills, competencies, and principles do not get taught in every school. I know how essential reading, math, social studies, and science play in developing a child's life. However, teaching reading, math, social studies, and science outside of workforce development will not create economic success. Education, outside the workforce context, is a form of schooling that can only create skilled, poor people. I know that you are not interested in being poor, or failing to realize your dreams, because you are reading this book. In the next several pages, you will find that Hustle Culture is your workforce coach and mentor that will help you create the future you want.

Teach Rules, Not Poverty

I know that I have your attention now! You are probably mad at your teacher, professor, and mentor because they did not teach you the rules you needed to succeed. It is not their fault. They were all taught the same information; they all have good intentions to make a difference in people's lives. They just do not know the rules; or they are so focused on academics that they neglected to remember that smart students will have to get a job one day!

I am not against anyone who writes books or creates programs focused on urban or disenfranchised communities' needs. The problem is that these books and programs simply scratch the surface of community and economic issues. They also teach subjects in isolation, not ever connecting them to the workforce context. On the flip side, I am not opposed to programs that focus on academically advanced students; these programs also fail to connect academia to the workforce context. These programs often give these students a false sense of security rooted in the idea that good grades result in a good job.

A great example of an epic failure in school is teaching young people personal finance outside of how to get and keep a high paying job. Another example is celebrating the ability of advanced students, while failing to cultivate their teachability, personal growth and risk taking. These young people thrive academically in high school and college, but often become mediocre in the workforce. They have degrees, but they lack the skills, competencies, and principles needed to compete in the job market.

You may feel this way. You may find yourself in a place where you are experiencing the aftermath of not being prepared to enter the workforce. You may be finding it difficult to leverage your life against poverty and social injustice. You are realizing that writing a resume, tying a tie, improving your credit, and dressing professionally are not enough; they are the outward expression but not the rules that govern the world of work. Please believe me, all is not lost. My desire for writing this manual comes from a need to energize and inspire you. Hustle Culture provides hope and solutions to change your experience in the workforce. **Hustle Culture is not just the game rules; it is the methodology and the rules of playing the game.**

This Manual Is for You

I wrote this manual for:
- **Every disenfranchised person**
- **Every high school student**
- **Every first-generation college student**
- **Every professional that just got a promotion**
- **Every prisoner that just got released**
- **Every person who just lost their job**
- **Every person who wants to start their own business**
- **Every teacher who wants to empower their students**
- **Every pastor who wants to empower their congregation**
- **Every youth program leader who wants to train the youth**
- **Every social service agency trying to facilitate change**
- **Every employer who sees the potential in an employee**
- **Every person with social, emotional, and economic barriers that have prevented them from going to the next level**

Hustle Culture is written for you!

Manual Organization

This manual consists of eight sections:

Section I-Introduction: The Dilemma
Section II-Leaving Grind to Find the Hustle
Section III-Welcome to Hustle Culture
Section IV-Hustle Culture the Paradigm Shift
Section V-Skills, Principles, and Competencies
Section VI-Hustle Mentality
Section VII-Hustle Transformation
Section VIII- Conclusion
Section IX-Resources

At this point in the manual, you have already completed Section I-The Dilemma. I challenge you to go through and read the entire manual first. Reading the manual first will help you absorb the Hustle Culture System and become familiar with the manual structure. You will find that there is a ton of information. I do not expect you to learn everything all at once!

After you read the manual one time; reread the manual, take notes, highlight, and implement the tools covered in this book and complete the workbook. Then reread the manual again; but this time, complete the book's activities and use the resources in the back of the book to further your learning. Uses markers and color pencils to personalize the pages of your book and make it your own.

Through this process, Hustle Culture will become a reference to which you can return and use to enhance your personal and professional growth.

Hustle Culture Is Not A Self-Help Book; It is a Battle Plan

Poverty is the most destructive force that plagues humanity. It is a gateway to other societal issues like crime, addiction, depression, and violence. For this reason, everything in this manual is a part of a personal battle plan for success.

When I start to discuss Hustle Culture with most people, they often have various excuses as to why Hustle Culture is not for them. Let's cut through the crap and agree that Hustle Culture is for you. If you come from a dysfunctional home and/or low economic situations that keep you from going forward, Hustle Culture is for you. If you have ever been underemployed and looking for work, Hustle Culture is for you. If you ever dreamed of starting your own company, Hustle Culture is for you! I am here to declare that Hustle Culture will help break through the barriers that keep you from going to your next level.

The question is not whether Hustle Culture is for you, but whether you will use what is inside of Hustle Culture. Will you apply what you read in this manual to your life? Will you conquer the oppression of fear? Will you pursue a lifestyle of Hustle Culture? If the answers to these questions are yes, then your life is going to change!

SECTION II: Leaving *Grind* to Find Hustle

In the early years of my journey, while I was developing the concepts of Hustle Culture, it was nothing for me to turn on my favorite playlist and get mentally prepared to *grind* it out. One day, I was sitting in front of my computer, getting ready to post pictures

that would show the world how much I was *grinding*, when I was overcome with a feeling of depression. I had two computers open, two phones, my Moleskine Journal, a calendar, and a huge cup of coffee. My ambitions had drained me; I realized that my life sucked. I was working sixteen to eighteen-hour days, had daily meetings, and a to-do list longer than the Bible.

On the outside, I was a young professional, with multiple degrees, a job that most people envied, a house, a wife, and a child. Underneath all of this, I was in debt, not sleeping, overweight and trying to convince everyone of my success. All my dreams were dying. The deeper relationships that I craved with the people that I loved were fractured and shattered. There I sat in front of my computer: burned out, lost, spiritually depleted, and unhappy. Even when I tried to meditate and pray, my mind was so messed up! I could only think about work and what I had to do next. I had driven myself to a significant breaking point. All I could do was hyperventilate and cry. I was a prisoner of a false perception of success and the victim of my daily *grind*.

After completely breaking down, my healing came when I reflected on my life. I had to come to terms with myself. Why was I *grinding*? Was I *grinding* for money? Was I *grinding* for power? The answer that came from within was medicine to my spirit and soul. The truth shocked me! I wanted to be popular! I wanted to be envied! I wanted to be the boss! I wanted to be that person others thought had it together! The fear of not wanting to disappoint the people around me was destroying my life. The reality was that I wanted people to accept me, not to reject me.

90% of my *grind* had nothing to do with me. The anxiety and the pressure of what I wanted others to think about me was destroying my life. I drove myself crazy because of my addiction to validation. Worst of all, I had no balance; I was losing myself in the process; and I was chasing prestige, power, position, and a paycheck.

Unfortunately, millions of people have felt like me, lost in the *grind* of life. Hustle Culture changed my life, and I was fortunate to make these changes early in my career. Most people work tirelessly and never see a lifelong return on their investment. They spend their entire life wasting away, working while their passions fizzle, and their goals become nothing more than daydreams. I decided early to change my life. I was working so extremely hard to be successful, but I found myself miserable and unsatisfied.

I developed Hustle Culture to be a toolkit to make it easier for you to enter the job market and create the life that makes you happy. Hustle Culture utilizes the energy that it takes to succeed and channels that energy into skills, competencies, and principles to develop you personally and professionally. If you use the tools in Hustle Culture, you will never find yourself unfulfilled in life or in your career.

See, when you are *grinding* and working, you quickly become an adrenaline addict who rushes after a calendar filled with stuff, fast-paced environments, meetings, and chaos. As a *grinder*, it is easy to get lost in proving your personal value to everyone while simultaneously forgetting to breathe, live, and fulfill your purpose.

Hustle Culture is not *grinding*; it is a lifestyle, ensuring that every action in your life reaps a valuable return on investment. Hustle Culture is about having skills, competencies and principles that allow you to live out your dreams while enjoying your life. **The topics in this manual will build your vision, create opportunities based on what you want to contribute to humanity, and guide you to enjoy your life.**

Hustle Culture is not a get rich quick strategy. The Hustle Culture tools do not change the time commitment needed to fulfill your purpose. You still have to put in the work and effort. The skills, competencies, and principles in this book are tools that you can use to work differently. These tools will teach you to leverage your time in order to get more work done and allow the time and energy to enjoy the things you value the most.

Hustle Culture does not replace the Universal Laws of Success. You still must have a vision for your life, a solid work ethic, the ability to stay focused, a passion for being a lifelong learner, and the courage to take advantage of opportunities. Hustle

Culture provides the pillars for the skills, competencies, and principles needed to live out your destiny and purpose in an environment where you are happy.

Winner Takes All

When I was *grind*ing, my mindset was all about "winning." Mentally, I focused on crushing my competitors and fighting my way to the top. A side effect of a *grind* mentality is the inability to become a better person. I spent more time trying to compete with someone else instead of being the best version of myself. Before Hustle Culture, I spent years analyzing my accomplishment instead of developing my authentic self. As a result of my futile efforts, I became a jealous hater and selfish. I could not accept people for who they were or what they had to offer; instead, all I saw was competition. I had eventually become a victim of my *grind*.

Hustle Culture is not about being a hater or jealous. It is about living in harmony with other Hustlers. In life, Hustlers respect the Hustle process, and they are authentically inspired to become themselves. They are dreamers that are committed to their vision. When you live a life based on your Hustle, your gifts and callings make room for you in the world.

No Sympathy

After reading my story above, you are probably wondering what this has to do with you and your situation. To you, I respond, "Everything!"

My story was about the lack of balance. People who *grind* are thirsty people - thirsty for opportunities and challenges that will lead them to fulfill destiny and purpose. People with a *grind* mentality are personally and professionally starved and thirsty. When you are thirsty, you will do anything for success; and in some cases, you are willing to lose or sell your soul. When you are workplace starved, you end up sacrificing family, love, and life to gain success. Hustle Culture is neither thirst nor starvation. Hustle Culture is a balanced approach to having abundance in both your personal and professional life.

Nothing in this manual will give you a shortcut to success—people who are successful work hard. If you want to change your life, you will have to put in time and effort. If you are reading this book and experiencing tough times, I empathize with you, but you have to fight back and keep going. Real success takes time, it builds character, and it develops grit. You may be feeling like you cannot take it anymore. I promise with Hustle Culture, you are going to Win! Do not lay down and accept your current reality; instead, keep punching. Hustle Culture is for individuals who have the grit to keep fighting. This manual shows you not only how to fight back; but, it teaches you how to change your combination of punches to better leverage your fight towards success.

Same Muscle, Different Mentality

Most people don't understand that there is a difference between the Grind and the Hustle. As you read this book, it is critical to understand that those who grind and Hustle often possess equal skill level, education, work ethic, ambition, connections, and mental muscle. However, their day-to-day movement in life is entirely different. Hustle Culture is about leverage and the advantage of having tools that you can use to master those movements, create wealth, and enjoy life.

As you dig deeper into this manual, and explore and apply the skills, principles, and competencies presented, you will transition from a thirsty grind mentality to a Hustle Culture. There are six components that combine to make Hustle Culture:

1. Hustle Culture is a Paradigm Shift with a strategic plan.
2. Hustle Culture is an educational curriculum focused on personal development, economic and workforce sustainability, and purpose.
3. Hustle Culture is built upon pillars of skills, principles, and competencies.
4. Hustle Culture is a philosophical approach to fulfilling purpose, vision, and mission.
5. Hustle Culture is a mentality that manifests itself through personal planning and action.
6. Hustle Culture is upheld by four construction laws- operational design, constructive implementation, and decorative interpretation.

Once again, Hustle Culture summarizes 20 years of personal experimentation as an educator, life coach, executive, and C.E.O. This Hustle Culture approach represents methods that I have learned and continuously practiced in my daily life. Embracing and incorporating the concepts in **Hustle Culture will take courage, focus, hard work, and a Hustle Culture Hunger Mindset (HCHM).**

Remember These Three Things

- **Number one**, *life is a personal journey. Your journey started on the day somebody conceived you. Everything that you need to complete this journey is inside of you.* My goal is to pull them out of you.
- **Number two** *never let any person, situation, or circumstance take control of your journey.* When you implement these concepts, you will have haters and people and situations will disappoint you. The key is to keep fighting.

- **Number three**, **you must have a Hustle Culture Hunger Mindset to grow into the Hustle Culture**. In Hustle Culture, it does not matter where you are today, stay hungry and go after your tomorrow.

Hustle Culture Hunger Mindset

As you begin implementing the manual's concepts, you will not master everything in the manual. This manual is full of information and resources that you will need to revisit daily, monthly, and yearly. I am coaching you to create a lifestyle. Creating a lifestyle will take a lot of practice, hard work, and time. The key is being hungry and consistent!

To achieve mastery, you will have to passionately pursue and diligently incorporate each new concept into your life. You must create new habits and passionately adhere to them. You must stretch yourself and commit to the latest patterns, routines, and self-improvement strategies outlined in the book. I encourage you to be consistent in this process, even when your Hustle appears not to be going well and when the results are not fast enough. Consistency is key when building your HCHM. I pledge to you that maintaining a HCHM will help you thrive. A Hustle Culture Hunger Mindset will also help you refine your Hustle and give you more momentum to keep pressing towards your vision.

I am confident that, regardless of whether you are a teen, a college student, a professional, a homeless person, or a prisoner, there is something in this manual for you. Let's Get It!

SECTION III-Welcome Hustle Culture

We all have a story

Hampton Runner

You have just been accepted to Hampton University. All the tutoring, lessons, clubs, activities, and athletics have paid off. Your parents are proud of you. Your father has

been waiting for this day. He worked overtime and saved every penny so that you can attend one of the most prestigious universities in the country. The problem is that you do not want to go to college, and you don't have the courage to tell him. The reality is that you want to see the world before you go to school. The only thing that you can see college doing is teaching you how to party. The stress has you to the point that you feel like running away after graduation.

Did My Time

You counted every second, minute, and hour of every day, year after year. You told yourself that once you got out, you would never return. The confinement, the danger, and the absence of love were enough to change your life. After years of legal fighting, you were finally released. Being released, however, could not retrieve the four years you lost being locked up. You now have a record and are a prisoner to the stigma associated with it. No one will hire you because of the time you have served. You

have no means of making money except for that which landed you in prison in the first place. The optimism that accompanied your freedom becomes dark because of your peppered past. What do you tell your 3-year-old when money gets funny and bills are due? What do you do with your vow never to go back to the streets?

Degree or not to Degree

It is now the end of your junior year at Howard University; you are an English major with a pre-law concentration. Your current G.P.A. is a 3.25, it could be higher, but you decided to pledge to a Greek Organization your sophomore year. You have had the time of your life in the last three years. You have met friends of all races, all creeds, and all colors. The parties, we'll just say, were "Off the Freakin' Chain!" You have bought t-shirts, jeans, compact disks, magazines, books, cell phones, coffee, and beer, way past the national average. You played video games until the controllers broke. You attempted to become a celebrity by uploading your college antics on YouTube©, only to arrive at the dawn of your senior year gearing to take the LSAT. Many people don't understand that practicing law is your family's legacy. You are supposed to be the third generation to take over the family firm. However, little does your family know that you dread the idea of practicing law. Little do they know that you are not going to law school. You want to become a camp counselor. The funniest thing is that you knew that you wanted to become a camp counselor at the start of your sophomore year after working all summer at Camp Unlimited, a camp for urban youth.

Family Matters

It is three days before graduation; you are the first in your family to graduate. The past two years since your mother's death have been challenging. While completing two rigorous years of school, you have been the sole provider for both you and your siblings. All your teachers tell you that you are so smart and have a bright future, but you know that your current economic and family situation leaves you disadvantaged. You have no clue what to do; you know you need to make money. You are incredibly talented but lack the knowledge and the mentoring to convert your talent into a living income. You just know that you need money to take care of you and your siblings. Anything other than employment is optional, including furthering your education.

Single Again

He said he would never leave you; that you would always be together and have a beautiful family. From the age of 17, he has been the only man you have known. After ten years of a marriage, one day you come home to find that everything is gone. You are left with only the clothes he left for you and your baby. You have spent your entire life chasing after him. You barely graduated High School, hardly found a job, and the income from that job is barely enough to cover your bills. You have no clue how to change your reality. You once had dreams of doing something great; those dreams did not entail being a single mother.

You're Fired

It's the week before Christmas, and you get terminated. You have worked diligently for this company for the past few years: you worked overtime, attended all meetings, never took a vacation, and never called off sick. Nevertheless, it was decided that the company would let people go due to production quality. H.R. and the Vice President decide to terminate your entire department. It is not as if you loved the job because you have a passion for something else; it's just that the job pays the bills. What are you going to do? You never had a job that paid you so well. What are you going to tell your family?

Unhappy

Your spouse has taken you to your favorite restaurant. You have just turned the magical age of 45. You find yourself reflecting on your life. You are married with two kids, two car notes, and a home that is worth $300,000. You are a senior manager at a fast-paced organization. You handle over $30 million worth of accounts; however, you are miserable. You have all this success, but there is a sense of emptiness that no one seems to understand. You live the picture-perfect life, but you fear that the worst has happened: you have not lived a life of purpose. When you tell all your friends that you feel like leaving your job to pursue your goal, they laugh. They inform you that you are going through a midlife crisis and should be satisfied with your ideal life. What will your spouse say? Will they support you, or will they divorce you or, even worse, send you to a mental hospital? You feel the pressure of living the status quo and fear making any economic changes because the bills keep rolling in month after month. You feel stuck and often find yourself hyperventilating. You only find peace when you entertain thoughts of getting in your car and driving away from it all.

Do any of these stories resonate with what is going on in your life? Have you been, or are you now in a similar situation? We all have a story! We all have faced challenges that make us want to give up or to make a drastic unpredictable change in our lives. For me, it was losing a lucrative job, getting divorced, becoming a single parent, and having to rebuild my life completely. I also had to deal with layers of trauma and poor decisions that led me to a place of unhappiness and regret. I did not like my story, so I fought to change it. You, my friend, can do the same thing. Before you run away from home, give-up on life, continue to lose sleep at night or leave your company, you must read this entire book! I understand that your stomach is in knots, and you are depressed because you are not living your best life. The time has come for you to suck it up and do something about it. It does not matter if you are in a penthouse suite or a prison cell; it is time for you to enter the Culture.

Hustle vs. *Grind*

The word Hustle sounds attractive, sexy, and exciting to anyone working hard in life. The fact of the matter is that Hustling should be appealing to anyone who feels compelled to live a life of endless and unlimited possibilities. In the last ten years, more people have become entrepreneurs, creatives, and carvers of their own paths to success. The reality is that we live in a time where nothing is impossible if you believe, know the rules, and are willing to work hard.

Niche Market Age

With the rapid changes in this new economy, we are currently living in a niche market age. **A niche market means that your product, service, talent, and skills are tailored to satisfy the need of a targeted demographic.** On a deeper level, who you are as a person and your contribution to humanity should fill a niche, regardless of if you are an employer or an employee. The fantastic thing about this niche age is that you can earn an income from your gifts and talents. The use of technology is creating more income-earning opportunities than ever before. Having a highly specialized niche is the key to success in this age. Hustling your gifts and talents in a niche market can create new industries.

Having a niche and finding personal success is using information and training for personal leverage. If you spend any time on the internet, you will find millions of motivational speakers, life coaches, sages, and success gurus all sharing their formula for success. This formula inspires, motivates, and trains their customers to find their niche. The problem is that most infopreneurs, or people who make money selling information, use the same formula for success. They all have the same recipe! The reason why they have the same formula is because personal development is a niche within itself which has its own market, rules and jargon. Consequently, to be successful, infopreneurs must play by the same rules and speak the same jargon.

Formula for Success

$$V+W+F+L+C=S$$
$$\text{VISION}+\text{WORK}+\text{FOCUS}+\text{LEARNING}+\text{COURAGE}=\text{SUCCESS}$$

The formula for success presented by most infopreneurs consists of having a vision for your life, a work ethic, the ability to stay focused, an affinity for learning, and the courage to take advantage of opportunities. While this formula is tried and true, it omits fundamental rules that enable the entrepreneur and creative to work smarter, not harder. Infopreneurs formula does not equip people with the skills, competencies, and principles needed to participate or excel in their niche. Infopreneurs formula neglects Hustle Culture!

$$HC\ (INPUT) = SFC\ (OUTPUT)$$
$$\text{HUSTLE CULTURE} = \text{SUCCESS}$$

Hustle Culture is the thinking engine behind all success formulas. Hustle Culture, in other words, is not a formula of success; it is the essence of success. It's the skills, competencies, and principles that when put into action (input), fuels their success formula (output). When you implement Hustle Culture, you start the systems of success in your life. Before we can proceed, let us define Hustle.

Definition of Hustle

Hustle is defined as the skills, principles, and competencies that an individual uses to purposefully move towards a clearly defined vision, with a sense of urgency and tenacity.

Hustle Culture is the 'way of life' that defines those individuals that Hustle. Hustle is the step-by-step system and action that channels the use of energy, time, skills, principles, and competencies to execute one's goals, mission, and vision. Hustle Culture is an integrated pattern of human knowledge, belief, and behavior that encompasses personal outlook, attitudes, values, morals, goals, and customs shared by those who Hustle (Entrepreneurs, Creatives, and Artist).

Hustle is not aimlessly doing stuff and making things happen. Hustle is about leveraging energy, time, skills, principles, and competencies to satisfy your mandate to accomplish your goals, mission, and vision.

The Hustle is the belief shared by people who are living their life based on a definite purpose. **If you are not focused and are not working daily to fulfill your goals, mission, and vision, you are not Hustling. If you are not leveraging energy, time, skills, principles, and competencies to improve your life, you are also not Hustling.** Hustling is so critical because we are not given forever to fulfil our dreams; instead, we are given a finite span of time to complete dreams that are infinitely huge. Hustling enables us to make the most of the time we are given.

The viewpoint behind Hustle Culture is that we exist in a universe that operates by time. Time does not discriminate. Time does not have a color; it does not belong to a particular socio-economic group of people. We all coexist in time. We all have time to make our dreams become a reality. The key to unlocking time is Hustle. Hustle is the manipulation of time to birth your vision for your life.

Most of us have never mastered the pillars needed to unlock time so we can open the door to our goals. Certain things are required to catapult us from *grind*ing into the world of the Hustle Culture.

Most people mistake grind for Hustle. The purpose of both is to achieve success; however, the process that each use is entirely different. For example, successful people possess an impeccable work ethic and focus. If you want to be successful, you will have to do the work; you have to implement the standard formula-vision, work, focus, learning, and courage; that is the foundation of success. The work does not change regardless of whether you are grinding or Hustling. The difference between grind and Hustle is the processes that you use by which you obtain that success.

Definition of *Grind*

Grind means to reduce to pieces. It is synonymous with the phrases "crushing it" and "killing it". Grind is a common expression used when someone is doing their job exceptionally well or pushing themselves to the limit to get things done.

The problem with building your success based on the grind is that grind is limited by time, energy, and talent. Grinding only benefits individuals that are naturally gifted in a particular area and have continuous high energy.

7Ft (*Grind*) vs. 6ft (Hustle)

I like to think of the Grind as a basketball player that is 7 feet tall. They are naturally more apt at dunking and excelling in basketball. Hustle, however, is a 6 ft basketball player who can dunk and play basketball just as well or better than the 7ft player.

Imagine both players in a dunk contest, based on height alone, and the 7-foot player has a natural advantage. However, the six-foot player leverages gravity and technique to the point that they overcome size deficiency to dunk the ball just as good or better than the 7ft player. The Hustle is about putting in both work (formula) while leveraging competencies, skills, and principles. To create results. You do not have to be 7ft with a

Hustle Culture to play the game; you must leverage skills, principles, and competencies to soar!

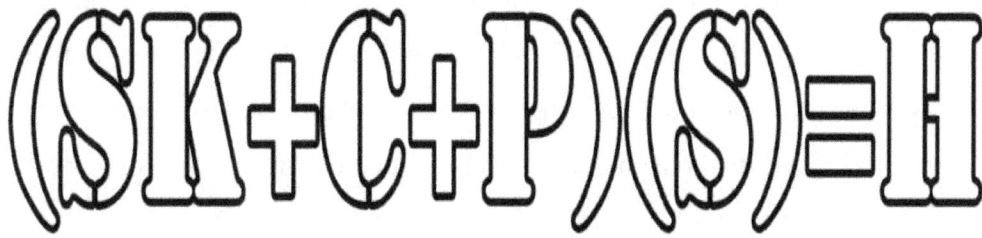

$$(SK+C+P)(S)=H$$

SKILLS+COMPETENCIES+PRINCIPLES X SUCCESS=HUSTLE

Time is a Commodity

The most significant limitation of grinding is time. When you are grinding, you may be making moves, but you do not use the time efficiently! Time is the only resource that is not renewable. You have a set amount of time in your life that you must use purposely and intentionally.

When you are grinding, it is extremely easy to neglect your values and purpose to become successful. The reason for the neglect is the urgency of time. When you are grinding, you do not have enough time in the day to get everything done. The following is a list of symptoms of grinding:

1. **You neglect yourself.**
2. **You fail to take care of your physical and mental health.**
3. **You measure your success by your work.**
4. **You do not take time to reflect on your wants and needs.**
5. **You stop having fun.**
6. **You stop standing up for the things that you believe in and your core values.**
7. **You stop being mindful**
8. **You stop taking risks and being innovative.**
9. **You neglect the people you love.**
10. **You settle for easy choices, negating the right decisions.**

Leverage your time to enjoy life, family, and the world around you, while fulfilling purpose in your life is Hustle Culture. When you spend your life in grind mode, you miss opportunities to become a better person, spouse, friend, and parent. You diminish critical chances to be reflective, creative, and opportunities to live in the moment. Hustle Culture is about making the right moves and mastering the proper positioning to have real prosperity, which is more time.

To leverage time and enter the world of Hustle Culture, you must reprogram your thinking. Hustle Culture is a paradigm shift that is a fundamental change in personal and professional development. Therefore, your beliefs about socio-economic status, education, and success must be redefined to build a Hustle Culture framework.

SECTION IV: Hustle Culture Paradigm Shift

The Prototype

My Dad came from humble beginnings. He was poor, black, and was the middle child of six. He was a child of a single mother and did not meet his biological father until he was forty. He spent most of his childhood in foster care, where he experienced neglect and abuse. This young man would grow up, get married, become a father, send me to college, become a pastor, and retire from a company that he worked for since he was twenty. What is your excuse? What is holding you back?

What is Your Excuse

We all have baggage and scars; some people, like my father, have more. While his story, like those of others, is unfortunate and horrific, he made a choice that reflected the idea that nothing in his past would stop him from creating a better life for himself and his family. **If you want to move to the next level, you must make a choice.** It is your

choice if you wish to make your life better. You can spend the rest of your life living in sorrow, making excuses, or you can get up and get it!

My Dad, a man filled with tough love, grit, and grind, is the foundation of the house that built Hustle Culture. He was kind and loving, but he had this mean fight in him that did not accept excuses. It was not until I entered the workforce that I understood the mindset he was trying to impart to me. A Hustle Culture Hunger Mindset!

Like my Dad, I have my gloves on. Welcome to ring! Welcome to Hustle Culture. I can only give you the knowledge that will help when you change. **At this point, your Degree means nothing; your professional accomplishments mean nothing.** What is essential are the skills, principles, competencies of Hustle Culture.

Fight Back

Poverty, as well as trauma, occurs among people of all ethnic backgrounds and in all countries. We all have a past; and, if we are living, we also have a future. So, get over yourself! You can be miserable, or you can bust a move. You can take the blows that life gives, or you can ball your fist and fight back. Life is humanity's biggest bully. It does not respond to passivity; it only responds to fighting faith. It surrenders to people who punch back!

Self-help books motivate and inspire you towards greatness. I am not here to motivate you. That's not Hustle Culture! If you were raised in extreme poverty, first-generation graduate, or a minority, your world is a dog fight. Life is systematically fighting against you as you pull your family out of generational systems of poverty. Contrary to what others think, you are not asking for pity or a handout! You don't need motivation; you need a plan. Hustle Culture is that plan.

Rich Folks Don't Teach Rules

Rich folks do not teach unwritten workplace rules. It is not because they are racist, nor do they dislike the poor; they are merely fighting for their survival as well. Workplace rules are hidden norms that schools fail to cover. These norms have been passed down, taught, and modeled by parents and family members. The ability to incorporate these rules often come from parenting, economic class, and culture. Therefore, to rich folks, Hustle Culture norms are to be followed since they are understood to be attached to family legacy.

Now think about family legacy and imagine a child that grows up in a home where their parents never had stable employment. They never saw their parent get up at a specific time and go to work. That child never observed their parent organize their day,

participate in a business meeting, email, or use the internet for business or personal development. Without intervention, that child is at a disadvantage when understanding simple elements of workplace norms. If you are that child, you are in the right place, and this manual is for you!

Paradigm Shift

What is the paradigm shift? The paradigm shift is the reconstructing of one's philosophy on socio-economic status, education, and success. To begin this reconstruction, we must begin with socio-economic status: There is no such thing as a middle class! Let me repeat; there is no such thing as a middle class.
The so-called "middle class" is a modern invention because the middle class is not actually connected to or defined by money.

The concept of a middle class is directly related to individual sustainability. Most people who would consider themselves middle class are members of a complex labor-class system. This system is based on certain values and individual sustainability.

From a purely economic and business perspective, you are either a laborer or an owner. It does not matter if you make 10k a year or 399k per year. If you sell your work for money, you are a laborer. If you make your money by owning land, businesses, housing, or banks, you are an owner. An owner's own things make them money, but the owner doesn't work for things that make them money. With actual ownership, you can make money 24hours a day, regardless of whether you are asleep or awake. This is the ultimate leverage of time.

The paradigm shift of Hustle Culture is to create a different mentality that builds on an individual's skills, competencies, and principles; and, helps them to transform their paradigm from that of a laborer to that of an owner. Hustle Culture is the cornerstone for growing an individual's capacity for individual sustainability; as well as, creating a new generation of owners.

Marginalization is Real

Wealth and poverty are connected to the systematic distribution of political, economic, and informational power. It is ridiculous to think that every person who lives in poverty is not working hard. It is also foolish to believe that poor people despise education, and they do not value money. The truth is that poor people and minorities have historically lacked access and exposure to distribution systems and opportunities that create generational wealth and sustainability.

The effect of this lack of exposure continues to self-perpetuate their socio-economic standing and their children's socio-economic standing for generations thereby creating instability. Hustle Culture provides the is the tools needed to develop personal and professional stability.

Hustle Culture Theory

If you want to survive in this new and every changing world you must have the tools that are more profound than how to tie a tie or how to slay an interview. *Your survival and stainability in the next 50 years will be based on your ability to be:*

- *Creative and innovative*
- *A critical thinker and problem solver*
- *A global communicator and collaborator*
- *Information and media literate*
- *A community and global leader*
- *Personal development focused*
- *Productive and accountable for your professional development*

At this very moment every industry is forced to focus on humanity's ability to survive. Survival is not just issue that we face on the National level, but it is also a International issue. Therefore, your niche or success in the marketplace is based on your ability to positively impact and develop solutions to human rights, inequality, humanitarian crises, and global sustainability. In this new economy, your impact on the world is more than the money that you will earn, it is connected to your ability to change the world.

Redefine Success: Hustle Culture

What person does not want the house, the car, and the clothes? The word Hustle has often associated with doing whatever it takes to make one's dreams come true. There is a fundamental thought that Hustling will make success happen; that Hustling will make "it", whatever it is, happen. I am *not* saying to go out into the world and not make it happen. Instead, I want you to redefine the "it" as the "success" you are going out to create. ***Hustle Culture Success is finding out what your purpose is in life, then educating yourself and developing the skills, competencies, and principles needed to fulfill that purpose.***

To be successful, you must be motivated by something more spiritual than money and tangible items. We all have varied needs; therefore, success is to be measured by the individual's fulfillment of those needs. It is "your" responsibility to determine what success looks like in your life. If you measure success by external approval and material things, then your success is flawed. The implementation of your purpose is the gauge of real success. This type of success is driven from within supersedes the opinions of others. Like my Dad used to say, "If you dream about being a trash man, be the best trash man you can be!" While trash collectors get paid well, the message is being your absolute best in the world.

Schooling Lie

The College Graduate

On June 8, 1997, I became the first male in my family to graduate from college. I can remember it like it was yesterday, the Dean of the College called my name and announced that I had completed my Bachelor of Science in Education.

What made that day even more exciting was that I was offered my first job the day before. The plan of going to college and getting a job was working; I was experiencing the American dream. My Dad tearfully looked me in the eye that day and said, "Son, you are now a man." He paid one month of rent and gave me $200. That moment changed my life. I graduated from the comfort of the college and entered into the real world, and it was not pretty.

I was an education major. While I had a job, I did not get paid until another three months. My Dad paid one month of rent, and I had to figure out how I would survive the three months before school started. During those three months, I spent several nights sleeping in my car with all my belongings. I eventually was blessed to stay with a friend, where I slept on the floor in an empty bedroom with only a pillow and a blanket. There was no turning back in my mind. I was 110 miles from home, and I needed to Hustle to survive. I found a telemarketing job and a retail job that helped me until I started my career.

The point of this story is that schooling did not prepare me for the real world. From June to September, my Degree meant nothing. In the next few pages, I will disclose the real purpose of education: it is the process that serves as a "Rites of Passage" in preparation to compete in the workforce.

The Biggest Deception

Unlike socio-economic status and redefining success, schooling is the biggest deception that enslaves the minds of people. While this statement may suggest that I am not for education, the opposite is true. I am a huge advocate of education and have spent and will continue to spend my entire life promoting and educating people; however, I am against the process of schooling. I believe that schooling and education are completely different. School and the schooling process systematically enslave the minds of people. At the same time, schooling destroys the educational process and the individual's ability to innovate and create. Let me explain why.

Schooling Defined

In 1828, Noah Webster defined schooling as "instruction in school." A school is a place where instruction occurs. The etymology of the word school is a place of leisure or a place free from work. The ultimate flaw of schooling is narrowing down what the instruction is supposed to be.

Education, however, is different. While "school" denotes a building that provides instruction, "education" means the formation of life. In 1828, Noah Webster defined education as follows:

n. [L. educatio.] The bringing up of a child, instruction; formation of manners. Education comprehends all that series of instruction and discipline which is intended to enlighten the understanding, correct the temper, and form the manners and habits of youth, and fit them for usefulness in their future stations.

Note that education is comprehensive. It deals with both the gaining of knowledge and the development of character and virtue. The combination of goodness and understanding leads to wisdom. Which in turn, ensures that the learning experience will prepare that individual for the future.

Over the last 20 years, schools have become big business. Millions of people are experiencing high tuition rates, coupled with low or underpaid employment opportunities. The life-long process of education has been substituted for expensive school experience. Our universities have become overpriced athletic and entertainment venues with shopping malls. Their focus is selling students an experience, not preparing them for a life of purpose.

As an educator with multiple degrees, I have participated in this schooling conspiracy and have given my students incorrect information. Like many teachers, I have told students that good grades and going to college would result in their ability to participate in the American Dream. I told my students that they would be able to buy a house, a car, go on vacation and get married, if they graduated and earned a degree. This misrepresentation of workforce culture led many of my students to choose degrees and certifications that now have no value in the marketplace. I did not educate my students, and many of them racked up an enormous student loan debt.

A 2019 Forbes article, *The New Your Federal Reserve*, confirms that college graduates between the ages of 22 and 27, holding a bachelor's degree or higher, are more likely to be unemployed and underemployed (Cooper, 2017). When they compared the college graduates to the overall working-class, these college graduates were stuck in temporary no-where jobs that paid extraordinarily little money. What was even more startling about the Forbes article was the 6% increase in unemployment for students with

a Liberal Arts Degree. Liberal Arts Degrees are degrees in arts, media, performing arts, ethnic studies, anthropology, and philosophy.

That simply means that schools are not teaching and aligning their curriculum to meet the needs of a future job market. The workforce numbers reveal that our systems of learning are not empowering or educating our children.

Today many of my millennial and post-millennials students are struggling to survive in a complicated global marketplace. In clear consciousness, I realized twenty years ago that we need less schooling and more education, because education provides an exodus out of poverty for students. Inspired by the essence of education, every lesson, activity, and program I implemented, from that moment forward, was intentionally designed to equip the student with a new world of understanding that would pave the way to their success. True education connects reading, math, social studies, and science to skills, competencies, and principles needed for workforce employment, both now and in the future. This is true sustainability!

The True Purpose of Education

Twenty years of my life have been devoted to studying, researching, and practicing in field education. What I discovered was that as educators, we have systematically lied to our students. We have taught for generations that *schooling* was the key to success. For an educator like myself, this whole idea about schooling was connected to the working-class fallacy and a false middle-class mindset. We lied to you, and I apologize! *The purpose of education is six-fold. Education is supposed to:*

1. Give you the fundamental knowledge on how to live your life.
2. Create a mental ecosystem by which you as a student can develop your Self-Esteem, Self-Worth, and Self- Confidence as you pursue your purpose.
3. Give you the knowledge to be able to become a functional person within society. (Reading, Writing, Math, etc.)
4. Help you develop a chronic processes and systems of learning how to learn.
5. Give you the civic knowledge to become thoughtful Citizens with the ability to participate in governmental process.
6. Give you the knowledge that will help you develop the skills, competencies, and principles designed for personal and professional development.

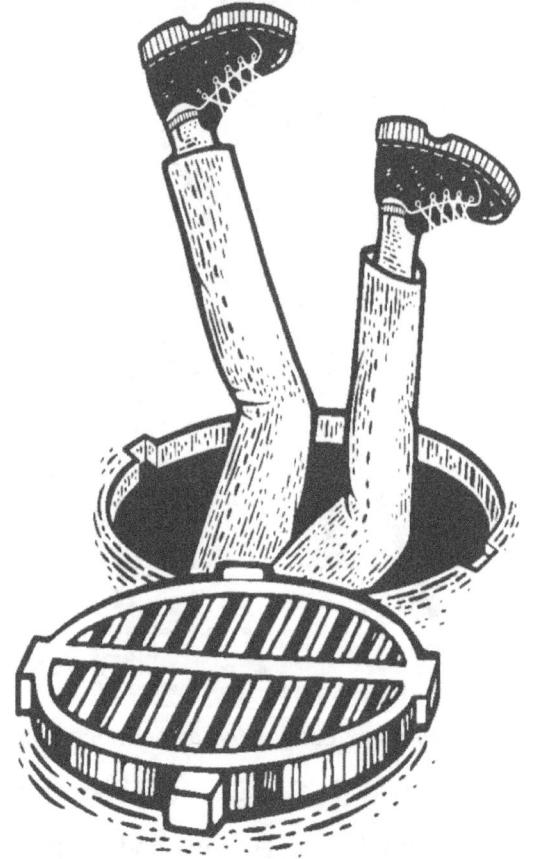

See, it wasn't until the housing crash of 2008 that I realized, without a shadow of a doubt, how true the premise of Hustle Culture was. Everyone was beginning to question the validity of the philosophical schooling system that clearly had failed the young adults were finding themselves drowning in student loan debt, unemployed and underemployed.

In 2008, I renewed my commitment to empower the next generation. I embarked on a renewed mission to fill in the gap by making Hustle Culture accessible to all those who felt left behind. Education had to be connected to the workforce development and a

Hustle Culture.

You Were Left Behind

In essence, traditional schooling has only resulted in continuous testing and a generation of students that struggle with creativity and problem-solving. At this very moment, millions of young people are set-up to become victims of future unemployment, underemployment, and insurmountable student debt. The reason for the epic failure is that schools are not teaching everyone the Hustle Culture Hunger Mindset. That is why you have this book! You are being called not only to be a champion, but a Hustle Culture Champion!

Hustle Culture Champion

I was raised in a working-class family. My father was a hardworking, blue-collar worker. My mom was the first person in her family to graduate from high school and college. I was the first male in my family to graduate from college. So naturally, I was taught to get a good education so I could obtain a good job. While I followed those rules, each year, I saw the rules change not only for myself but also for my peers.

In the early '90s, the marketplace became incredibly competitive. Year after year, a degree became only one aspect of the employment criteria. By the time I had graduated from college, I had to change my philosophy about life and education because my success depended on it, and my survival demanded it. I had to combine the grind mentality that my father had with my mother's intellectual fortitude in order to Hustle and survive in a ruthless job market. When I combined grind with intellect, I became a Hustle Culture Champion.

While writing Hustle Culture, I discovered that education was not the determining factor in securing employment. While a diploma and credentials are vital for getting an interview, they do not guarantee a job. However, self-discovery and purpose give you an advantage over most candidates. The more I could articulate my skills, competencies, and principles throughout my career, the more valuable I was to the organization.

As I went from a classroom teacher to an executive, the learning curve I experienced was that the working-class rules did not give me a competitive advantage. In my field of work, everyone has a diploma, Degree, or training; therefore, what separated me from everyone else was my mastery of specific skills, competencies, and principles, while having a working portfolio of experiences that showcased them in action. Degrees, diplomas, and employment do not work synonymous with each other. If you fail to recognize this truth, you will fall into a group of people I call the working poor. The working poor is a group of schooled, unemployed or underemployed people.

Education is not designed to get you a good job! That's Right! Your parents, your teacher, and even the media have lied to you. Education is designed to teach you how to think, solve problems, and create.

If you are an employer reading this book, think of how many of your employees are not self-starters? How many people do you employ who avoid taking the initiative in hopes for you to tell them what to do? Think about individual employees who lack confidence in their decision-making and problem-solving skills. Many of them are smart and articulate, but they lack grit, grind, and Hustle; consequently, they crack under pressure.

With the current global economy, Fortune 500 Companies are not only looking for individuals with degrees, but they are also looking for individuals who benefit the organization. They are looking for a Hustle Culture Champions. They are hiring individuals who bring something unique to the organization that will increase wealth. **They are not looking for people who play by the rules; they look for innovators who create new games.**

Everything you bring to the job market is essential. Your life, culture, skills, and experience make you a resource to companies and the global marketplace. The cool thing is that companies, organizations, and people are willing to pay top dollar for what you can contribute. However, they are not as generous and sometimes reluctant to pay for that graduation piece of paper. Unlike former generations, the current workforce is driven by who you are, not what you are. Workforce success is knowing who you are, what you believe, and what gifts and talents you bring to the table.

The facts are that 90% of all high paying jobs (100k or more) are based on critical thinking and problem-solving skills. If you master these skills, you can quickly become a resource for any organization.

Back to the Foundation

The remainder of this manual is an instrument used to authenticate and cultivate a person's individuality. You will find tools and resources that will help you discover your individuality and identity.

Hustle Culture is true education derived from the word edco, which means to empower or bring out the full potential. The whole purpose of Hustle Culture is to help you reach your full potential. You are born with an innate perfect operating system. **Your "Human O.S.", or "Human Operating System", comes with courage, the desire to learn, love, explore, create, and discover.** We are programmed to be individually great with the ability to innovate and create. Our inward hardware is damaged through improper programming. The program failure comes from poor schooling, parenting, and the life's peaks and valleys. I created a Hustle Culture to fix the wrong programming.

Here is the Point

If you believe that your certificate, diploma, or Degree will guarantee success, you are probably just entering the workforce, unemployed, and/or underemployed. If you believe that success is solely money, you are probably unhappy and miserable. This section exists to confront the lie and the misconceptions that keep most people from growing. These misconceptions are thoughts of personal entitlement, socio-economic entitlement, and educational entitlement.

Ownership of Learning

In the next section, you will be exposed to tools and principles that alter your life: the skills, competencies, and principles that encourage you to release creativity, discovery, imagination, and self-exploration.

SECTION V-Skills, Competencies, and Principals

    Clear your Mind! At this very moment, your certificate, your diploma, and your degree mean nothing. The twelve to twenty plus years of time and financial investment in school you have exchanged for a $2 piece of cardstock, laced with expensive ink and stickers, positioned in a faux leather case. Think of yourself as rookie! You have not arrived; you have only participated in the preseason of your career aspiration. Today, your educational accomplishment means nothing! Your title is worthless! You are about to enter the Hustle Culture Arena. An octagon filled with optimism, hope, risk, and endless opportunities. The Hustle Culture Arena is the place champions are born.

    In the realm of Hustle Culture, education, titles, experience is subservient to productivity! This section is the blueprint of Champions. It covers the skills, competencies, and principles that will differentiate you from the other victims holding $2 piece of cardstock. In order for this section to wake up the sleeping Champion inside of you, you must shake yourself from the false self-worth and security that you attach to your degree, diploma, or certificates. You must see your value through the lenses of productivity and not your title. Before you step into the arena, think about these questions:

1. **What do you contribute to the world?**
2. **Why should someone hire you, or patronize your business?**

Survival in this Culture is based on being an asset to both your organization and your community. Your ultimate value is based on the skills, competencies, and principles that you possess. This section will cover the essential skills, competencies, and principles that everyone needs to participate in Hustle Culture. I call them the Hustle Culture Pillars.

Before you even think about leaving your job or starting a business, you must learn to incorporate and apply these Pillars because they are critical to your survival and are the keys to your success. These Pillars support the Hustle Culture Arena, and they are critical to you achieving your dreams and purpose.

Pillar 1-Hustle Culture Skills

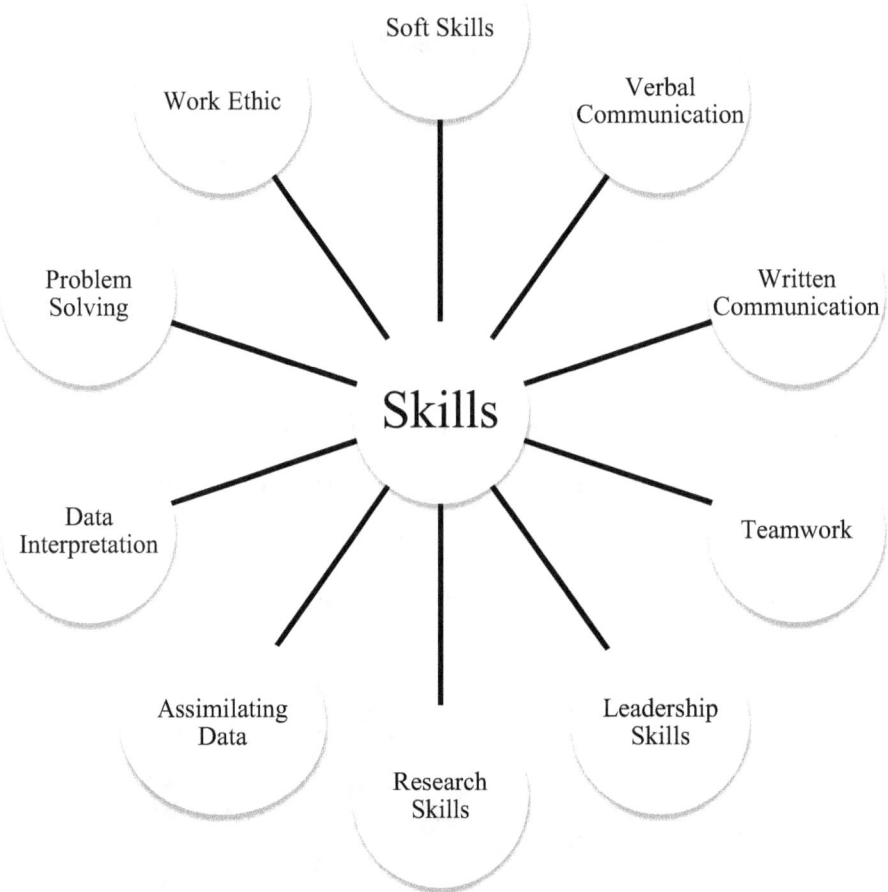

If you have attended school in the last thirty years, you have probably heard about workplace skills, career skills, or life skills. I like to call them Hustle Culture Skills. These are skills that are non-technical or job specific. Hustle Culture Skills can be used in any profession, vocation, industry, or business. These skills are critical in helping you thrive in the workforce. Hustle Culture Skills are fundamentally crucial to preserving your job, achieving career advancement, and procuring and maintaining clients and customers.

Everyone can be taught how to do a job, but it takes skills to have a strategic advantage and keep a job. According to Harvard University's *"Pathways to Prosperity Project"* study in 2011, U.S. employers see an increasing number of University graduates unequipped to survive in the 21st-century workforce. The problem is that these students are struggling in the workplace, or they lack Hustle Culture Skills. This skill deficiency is the result of these skills not being taught.

Note: The proceeding skills could be considered a manual within themselves; for this reason, more information regarding these skills can be found at www.gpunlimitedco.com, Kaperkins.com or hustlecultureco.com.

1. Work Ethic

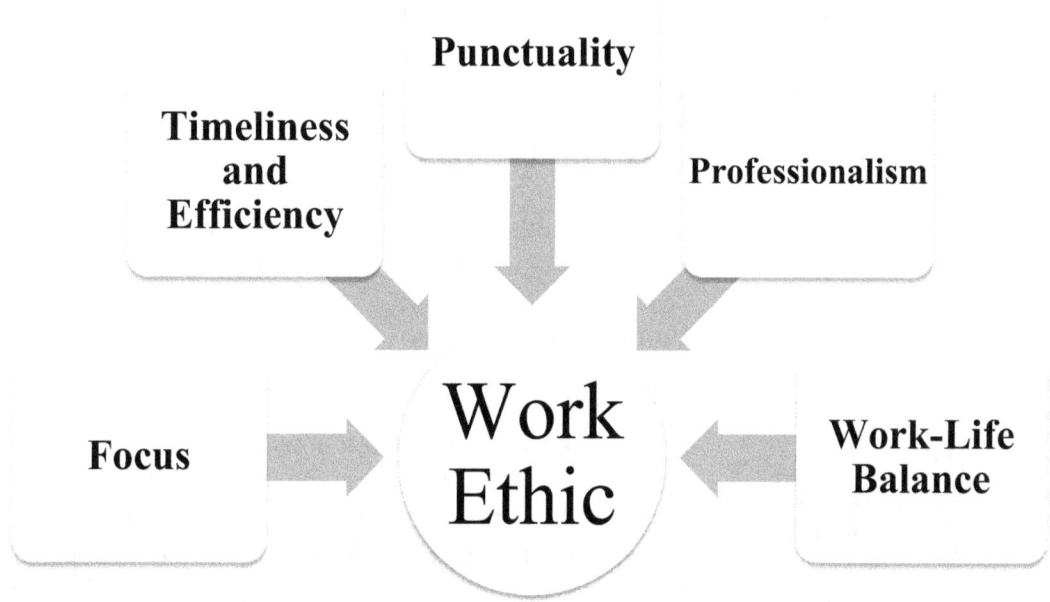

The discussion of Work Ethic is a daunting task because every organization has their own culture by which products and services are produced. In the Information Age, there is a significant difference from company to company about the idea of Work Ethic. However, as a former supervisor, executive, and current C.E.O., work ethic is an identifiable value system. Work Ethic is a set of principles to which you hold yourself accountable. It is the quality of effort exerted to perform a task or deliver a service. It is a culmination of persistent diligence, thoroughness, and self-motivation. Work ethic is often displayed in the quality of work that is produced on a constant basis. Below we will the five things that will improve your Hustle Culture Work Ethic: focus, timeliness and efficiency, punctuality, professionalism and work life balance.

A. Focus

If you ever have an opportunity to spend a day with a C.E.O. or Executive of any organization, one thing you will find is that many of them have an unbelievable amount of focus. They will keep going as long as necessary to get the job done. In their world, the *Hustle* is Real; therefore, the focus is mandatory. Eating, sleeping, breaks, using the restroom, entertainment, and socializing is optional. Executives are mental marathon runners who have developed over time the mental and physical stamina by which their spirit, soul, and body come into complete alignment to fulfill a needed objective. This level of focus does not happen overnight. To develop this level of attention requires ongoing training. It takes time to train your mind and body to work for extended periods with extreme focus. There are five things that you can do to increase your focus.

i. Assess Your Level of Focus.

If you daydream, lose track of time in the middle of a task, and are easily distracted, then you have horrible focus. If you want to excel, take the time to fix your focus.

ii. Eliminate Distractions

Learn to eliminate distractions. If you are married and or have children, these are not distractions. These are personal responsibilities that you must manage and steward. These are responsibilities that require you to reserve time to engage with the people you love. Everything else should be considered a distraction. Not all distractions come from outside sources (i.e., people). Exhaustion, worry, anxiety, low motivation, and other internal disturbances can be particularly tricky to avoid when it comes to focusing.

iii. Focus on One Thing

Recent studies have shown that multitasking is a myth. Research shows that the brain cannot complete more than one complex task at a time. This would include attempting to do two or more jobs simultaneously, switching back and forth between tasks performing several tasks in rapid succession. The negative results of multitasking are startling. Research suggests that multitasking damages your short-term memory. It can increase anxiety, decrease creative thinking and increase mistakes. When people divide their attention between multiple tasks at once, they are doing less work, experiencing more stress, and performing worse than those who only focus on a single task.

iv. Create a Daily Plan with Dedicated Time for Focused Work

Plan! It is that simple. Your plan is your blueprint for your day. It holds you accountable for everything that you attend to accomplish during the day. Your plan is also your first line of defense against multitasking. You should have in your schedule a non-negotiable focused time of work. You should also schedule a time to check your email and to take breaks. Most importantly, your daily plan should be scripted.

v. Other Options

Other options to help you focus include optimizing your workspace by removing clutter so that your mind can focus. I also suggest blocking distracting websites when you want to focus. In the appendix, I have provided a list of apps to use if you are on the computer a lot. Once again, the goal is to limit the urge to multitask. So, notifications, content switching, and social media can be huge distractions.

B. Timeliness and Efficiency

People with a fantastic work ethic do not procrastinate. They have intense focus and immediately do whatever it takes to accomplish a task. In addition to completing a task promptly, your Hustle Culture Work Ethic completes the job with excellence. When your work is not efficient, people will question your ethics and professionalism.

C. Punctuality

To make a good impression on people, you should always be punctual for school, work, or appointments. The rule is 10 minutes is early and 5 minutes is on time.

D. Professionalism

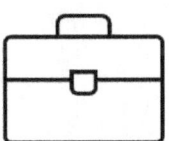

Being a professional is more than wearing business attire. Professionalism is a mixture of workplace demeanor, attitude, and values. It is essential that you practice being cordial and positive. Never partake in any form of gossip. Professionalism includes both on the job and in your personal life. Professionals are respectful of others' lifestyles and work to develop a reputation for being an honest, hard worker.

E. Work-Life Balance

While it is essential to show your employer that you are willing to work hard, it is crucial to create a healthy work-life balance. Hustling too much can cause you to become overwhelmed and tired, changing your Hustle to grind. Therefore, it is vital that you schedule a time to relax and rest.

2. Soft Skills

Soft Skills

Communication
Writing
Relationships
Phone /VoiceMail
Email
Computer
Customer Service
Creativity
Organization
Time Management
Networking
Appearance
Etiquette
Integrity
Adaptability

Soft Skills are skills that are needed to function day to day in the real world. Soft Skills are mandatory, regardless of whether you are an employee or an employer. Soft Skills are a combination of people skills, social skills, communication skills, character or personality traits, attitudes, career attributes, social intelligence, and emotional intelligence, etc., all of which are included as another Hustle Culture Skill. Soft Skills enable you to navigate your personal and professional environment.

A. **Effective Communication Skills:**

Emotional Intelligence	Active Listening	Non-verbal Communicatio	Clarity	Summarizing
Empathetic	Feedback	Trust and Rapport	Being Present	Friendly

Effective communication is a dynamic process. It is one of the Hustle Culture Skills that must be practiced. How you communicate can affect your Hustle outcomes and relationships. It is through communication that we exchange or impart information to each other. Communication conveys what we feel, what we think, and what we believe. Therefore, communication is essential for effectively conveying information in both written and oral forms. Ten practical communication skills give you a competitive advantage when you communicate thoughts and ideas:

1. **Emotional Intelligence**- Emotional Intelligence is your ability to manage your emotions when you communicate a message. It is vital that any messaging given to people is void of perceived emotions. Therefore, it is critical that the messenger is self-aware, self-managed, and socially aware of both the context and content.
2. **Active Listening**- Active Listening is the ability to listen intently and effectively. It is important to listen to what other people are saying, as opposed to thinking about how you are going to respond.
3. **Non-verbal Communication** – Great communication is more than what you say, but it is connected to the non-verbal way of saying it. This can include the use of eye contact, facial expressions, posture, and tone. Excellent communication gives you an advantage; therefore, it is critical that you are aware of the signals that you are sending; what you say can be miscommunicated nonverbally.
4. **Clarity**- Before you start any conversation or discussion, either oral or written, you must have a purpose. Are you trying to obtain information? Are you trying to convince the audience? If communication lacks clarity, it can create confusion.
5. **Summarizing**- a form of communication that is critical to hearing what is actually being said, not your interpretation. After every conversation, it is essential that you reflect and summarize what you have heard from the other person. Summarizing is another way to enhance your active listening and to ensure that you have the correct message.

6. **Empathetic**- Empathetic communication is the communication that shows your ability to understand and share the feelings of another. This form of communication can give you a strategic advantage and influence. Empathy allows you to settle disagreements, develop synergy, and win colleagues, partners, and customers.
7. **Feedback**- In the day-to-day Hustle, you can often lose sight of how valuable feedback can be. I have learned that honest, positive, and constructive feedback is key to individual and organizational success. Feedback improves performance, creates a pipeline of professional and personal growth. It builds employee and customer loyalty. It increases business outcomes, and most importantly, it drives performance.
8. **Trust and Rapport** -Do people trust you? Has your communication fostered relationships or hindered them? Can people trust you to deliver on promises based on your word? If the answer is no, then you have some work to do.
9. **Being Present**- No matter how hectic your day is or how stressful times may be, are you present in every conversation. Being present in a meeting means thoroughly engaging in the moment. Engaging with the audience, focusing and

listening is being present. When you have conversations with others, are you focused on the speaker, or something else?

10. **Friendly**-What is the tone of your message? Is your communication personalized? The most crucial thing in excellent communication is to ensure that the message is customized to the listener. Making generalizations about people can be disrespectful and offensive.

B.   Industry Writing

It is critically important that you understand and are able to communicate the language of your chosen industry. It does not matter how naturally gifted you are in your chosen industry; if you cannot share information in your industry's language, you will not be able to navigate your particular industry niche. Industry language is a clear indication of learning, expertise, and mastery of your chosen craft. For example, a web designer should be knowledgeable of terms like HTML, C.C.S., and PHP. A teacher should know about lesson plans and IEPs. Business professionals should know about profit and loses.

C.   Workplace Relationships and Demeanor

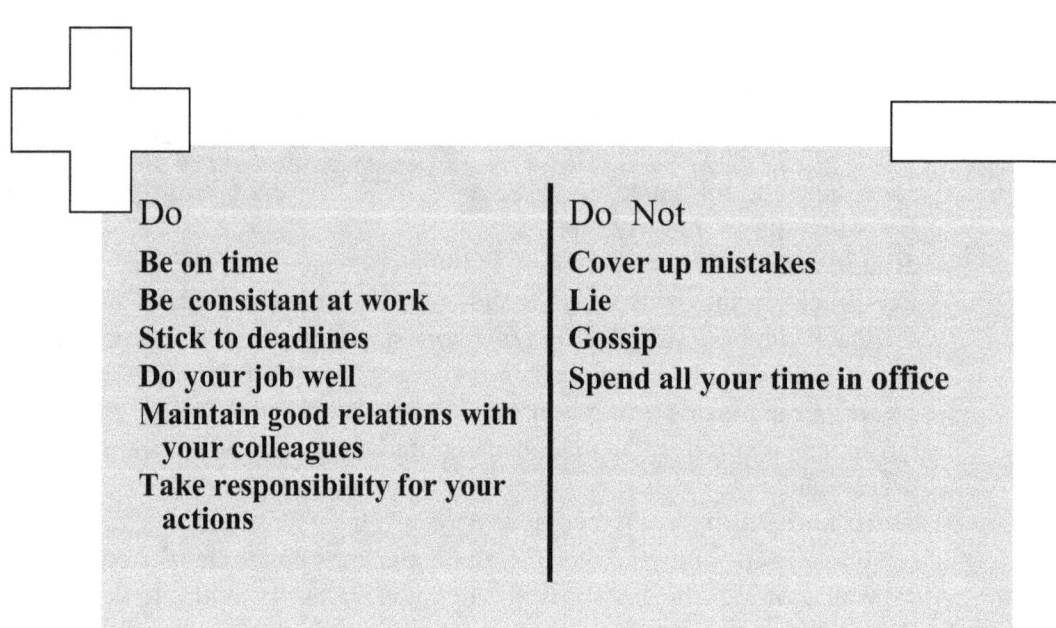

Do	Do Not
Be on time	**Cover up mistakes**
Be consistant at work	**Lie**
Stick to deadlines	**Gossip**
Do your job well	**Spend all your time in office**
Maintain good relations with your colleagues	
Take responsibility for your actions	

Workplace relationships and demeanor are essential. What does your personality, attitude, behavior, professionalism, and communication say to coworkers, subordinates, superiors, and customers? Does your workplace mentality reflect passion and optimism? Workplace demeanor can be very tricky because outside of work culture, perception is not always reality. However, in work culture, perception is reality. What people perceive is critically important to ensure your ability to have a Hustle Culture Advantage. Your workplace messaging is connected to profit and production; therefore, it is critically important that you spend the time and resources needed to ensure that your reality aligns with the message you want to convey. Workplace messaging will help you develop professional relationships with people.

The real test of your workplace demeanor is how you perform when your life is not going so well. Will you go to work? Will you allow issues to impede your performance? As I have stated, the workplace culture can be brutal. Bringing your problems to work is unacceptable. Hustle Culture demands that regardless of what is going on in your life, you must produce.

No one wants to work for, or hire, a negative or unprofessional person with a bad attitude towards their job, colleagues, and customers. If you do not have anything to say positive, then do not say anything. If you have comments with no benefits or solutions, it might be better to remain silent. Be careful of your tone. Tone refers to how you modulate your voice or the change in your pitch. Tone makes up 38% of our communication.

If you are new to any organization, unless you are hired as a consultant or an executive officer, spend the first six to twelve months learning the organization's culture. Instead of running your mouth and volunteering your opinions as a newbie. Take time to learn the people and the culture in order to more effectively foster relationships with key stakeholders. You will find that you do not have to volunteer your opinion; it will be solicited.

D.   Phone and Voicemail Etiquette

It is important to effectively represent your organization on the phone. Phone and voicemail etiquette are very vital. Using phone phrases such as thank you and please is indispensable in a professional environment. Maintaining, checking, and responding promptly to voicemail is also especially important in this fast-paced Hustle Culture.

E. **Email Etiquette**

In the age of technology, the use of email is essential in a professional environment. However, many people have lousy netiquette. When you are overwhelmed with meetings and projects, email can seem like an easy fix to communication. However, lousy netiquette can cause more harm than good.

In many cases, we should pick up the phone and call. When projects are complex and need to be explained, email is not the right medium to convey the message. Emails should never be used for last-minute cancellations of meetings, lunches, interviews, or sharing devastating news.

As a rule, all corporate email accounts are always used only for work purposes (Even If You ARE THE OWNER). There are at least 40 rules that will easily correct your email etiquette quickly if you implement them today. These are simple rules that you must follow when writing useful emails.

40 Email Rules to Remember

- Be concise and to the point
- Answer all questions, and preempt further questions
- Use proper spelling, grammar & punctuation
- Make it personal
- Use templates for frequently used responses
- Answer swiftly
- Refrain from sending unnecessary files
- Use proper structure and layout
- Do not overuse the high priority option
- Do not write in CAPS
- Do not leave out people in the message thread
- Add disclaimers to your emails
- Never Email angry or stressed
- Read the email before you send it
- Always briefly introduce yourself
- Do not overuse reply to all option
- Mailings the bcc: field or do a mail merge
- Do not use abbreviations, emojis, jargon, and slang
- Be careful with formatting
- Make sure all emails have a signature
- Do not forward chain letters
- Refrain from sending one-liners
- Do not request delivery and read receipts
- Do not ask to recall a message; send a new email and indicate your mistake.
- Refrain from copying a message or attachment without permission
- Do not use email to discuss confidential information; make a phone call
- Use a meaningful subject
- Use active instead of passive
- Avoid using URGENT and IMPORTANT
- Avoid long sentences
- Refrain from sending or forward emails containing libelous, defamatory, offensive, racist, or obscene remarks
- Do not forward virus hoaxes and chain letters
- Keep your language gender-neutral
- Do not reply to spam
- Use cc: field sparingly
- Only discuss public matters
- Use your work email for work
- Make sure the subject line matches the message
- Send only two attachments
- Make sure you warn the reader of large attachments

Note: Your email reflects you. Every email that you send adds to or detracts from your reputation and your demeanor.

F. **Computer Etiquette**

Never Save Personal Files to Your Desktop	**Never visit Any website that is not Job Related**	**Never Have Personal Conversations Over Office Chat**
Never Shop Online	**Never Use Your Personal Email**	**Never Search for Jobs at Other Companies**
	Never Use Your Social Media Account On Your Work Computer	

I will not go into detail about computer etiquette; only use your work computer for work. I understand that many people use the work computer for personal projects. It is in poor judgment to use the work computer to pay bills, check private messages on social networks, browse the web, download, and live multimedia. That is a professional no-no. It may be convenient but never do it! Many companies have servers or systems that monitor use, so be very cognizant about that. What you look at on a corporate network can be used against you.

If you are a techie and are addicted to media, social networks, blogs, and emails, I recommend purchasing phones with internet and data plans that allow you to stay connected. However, even then, refrain from doing personal business on corporate time. As an entrepreneur, your business deserves your attention; it is essential to utilize a specified computer for your business. This will help you develop the mental discipline to disconnect your business from your personal life. Respecting your time and your business affairs must become a skill that you incorporate. Even as a C.E.O. of my own company, I have learned that I must set time aside to complete business-related tasks and time aside to complete personally related tasks.

B. Customer Service

Answer the phone (i.e., smile, say hello, and tell them with whom	Don't make promises you can't keep	Know your products, services and company	Listen and take the time to know your customers
Deal with complaints	Be helpful – even if there's no immediate profit in it	Never argue with the customer, be courteous and knowledgeable	Take the extra step and always over-deliver
	Throw in something extra if you can	Commit to quality and integrity	

Customer service is the process of responding to the needs of your company's clients. The general belief of all industries is that customer satisfaction is important. The customer is always! Your object, regardless of whether you are an employee or an employer, is to keep the customer satisfied and coming back.

It is critical when you are relating to customers that you incorporate being polite and professional. There are ten simple rules of fantastic customer service:

1. *Answer the phone (i.e., smile, say hello, and tell them with whom they are speaking).*
2. *Do not make promises you cannot keep.*
3. *Know your products and industry.*
4. *Listen and take the time to know your customers.*
5. *Deal with complaints.*
6. *Be helpful – even if there is no immediate profit in it.*
7. *Never argue with the customer, be courteous and knowledgeable.*
8. *Take the extra step and always over-deliver.*
9. *Throw in something extra if you can.*
10. *Commit to quality and integrity.*

Fantastic customer service is not a tactic, but it is a mentality. It takes time and effort to create great customer experiences.

H. Creativity

In every industry, it is beneficial for you to think outside the box. The global economy is competitive, unstable, and uncertain. Academic qualifications and job experience are important, but innovation and creativity create workforce sustainability. If you can effectively and efficiently complete job associated tasks, while also contributing a different perspective, creating new or improving upon products and processes, then you become an asset to your industry.

Creative thinkers are in global demand and become assets to the global economy.

Companies and customers are willing to pay more for creativity for these four reasons:
1. *Creativity increases efficiency and effectiveness.*
2. *Creativity brings solutions that can save money, increase profitability, uncover unresolved issues, and find niche market opportunities.*
3. *Creativity expands the corporate reach and global branding.*
4. *Creativity fosters broad thinking and alternative outlooks.*

I. Organizational Skills

Organizational skills are personal management systems that you use to get things done. These are the systems that you use to govern your life and your time. Organization skills may include, but are not limited to, your ability to manage your time, use of a calendar or planner, and your ability to prioritize tasks. Organizing is not the organization of multiple tasks, it is the organization of which tasks get priority. You don't want to multitask because it is not efficient, as discussed earlier.

If you look at employment websites like CareerBuilder®, Indeed, and Monster, you will find jobs with various responsibilities. If you are an entrepreneur, you must handle multiple tasks and multiple projects. These responsibilities, tasks and projects can only be accomplished by having organizational skills. You must possess the ability to prioritize numerous tasks and projects.

Organizational skills are all about efficiency and production. Hustle Culture is about doing more, being faster, and delivering results with fewer resources and time. Therefore, you must organize properly to get the most out of your day. Here are some helpful tips:

1. *Always have a calendar.*
2. *Avoid unintentional task-switching (Multi-Tasking). It eats time.*
3. *Do not leave your house without planning your day.*
4. *Schedule and compartmentalize time to address unexpected interruptions and issues.*

5. *Reduce all meetings to 45 min. Regular meetings are normally set in 1hour time increments. Having shorter, more concise meetings will add time back to your day, in some cases, up to two months' worth of time.*
6. *Block off time in your calendar for breaks and/or power naps.*
7. *Work off-site if you have an opportunity.*
8. *On mobile devices, consolidate the places you need to go for information.*
9. *Disable all pop-up notifications on the phone and computer.*
10. *Schedule time for checking emails.*

Below, I have provided tools that you can use to organize your Hustle better:

Project Management Software Click Up Asana Trello	**Document Cloud Storage** Dropbox Google Drive Box	**Note Taking** Keep Evernote Simple Note
Work Automation Zapier ntegromat Automate.io	**Day Planner** Moleskine Franking Covey Disc Binders Leverenge	**Journal** Moleskine BooQool **Leuchtturm1917** Minimalism
Index Cards /Sticky Notes	**Sticky Notes**	**Writing Tools** Pens Pencils Higlighters Permant Markers

J. Time Management

People often merge time management with organizational skills; however, time management is really different form organization. Time management is how you schedule your time. It is how you manage or fulfill your goals and objectives in a measured number of minutes and hours. You are relied upon to get a specific amount of work finished in an assigned period of time. Take time to think about what you need to accomplish and arrange your schedule based on their importance. Use your time first to complete the most important things, then work your way down the list. If you spend too much time on the first item, you may never get to the second item, so plan your time and day well. Refrain from activities that derail your focus and concentration. Non-productive activities can include casual work socialization, using social media, extended breaks, and mental wandering. **The following is a list of online software applications that you can use to leverage time. These tools range from note taking, project management, social** media management and document creation.

Simple Tools To Use To Leverage Time	
• nTask	• ProofHub
• Trello	• Celoxis
• Clickup	• Time Doctor
• HubSpot CRM	• Wunderlist
• ProjectManager.com	• Google Docs
• Asana	• Pinterest
• Dropbox	• MS OneNote
• Google Drive	• XMind
• Box	• Leuchtturm1917
• Evernote	• Minimalism
• Google Keep	• Index cards
• Simplenote	• Sticky Notes
• Process Street	• Logaster Profit Margin Calculator
• PerfectForm	• TeamViewer
• LogicGate	• Horizon 7
• Notion.so	• ConnectWise
• Slite	• Diigo
• Confluence	• Calendly
• Zapier	• Jour
• Integromat	• Panda Planner
• Automate.io	• Simple Elephant
• Bubbl.us	• Airtable
• MindMeister	• Office 365
• Lucidchart	• Google Suite

K. Networking

Networking Check List
✓ **Professional Attire**
✓ **Leather Portfolio with all marking materials**
✓ **Business Cards**
✓ **Promotional Materials**
✓ **Note Card for documenting referrals and connections**
✓ **Something to write with**

Networking brings about professional growth and partnerships. The process of networking is about building relationships and exchanging resources. Author Lauren Neilson, Director of Small to Medium Enterprise Growth, defines networking in her article, *Eight Tips to Help You Become a Networking Guru,* as "the bringing together of like-minded individuals who, through relationship building, we become walking, talking advertisements for one another (Neilson)."

1. Have networking tools with you. Networking tools include but are not limited to having business cards and brochures about your business.

2. Set a goal for the number of people you will meet. Identify a reachable goal based on attendance and the type of group. If you feel inspired, set a goal to network with 15 to 20 people, and make sure you get all their business cards.

3. Act like a host, not a guest. A host is prepared to do things for others, unlike a guest who sits back and relaxes. Volunteer to help greet people. If you see visitors sitting, introduce yourself, and ask if they would like to meet others. Act as a connection between people.

4. Listen and ask questions. Remember that a good networker has two ears and one mouth and uses them proportionately. After you have learned what another person does, tell them what you do. Be specific but brief. Do not assume they know your business.

5. Don't try to close a deal. These networking events are not to be a vehicle to solicit colleagues to buy your products or services. Networking is about developing relationships with other professionals to expand your range of influence. Meeting people at networking events should be the beginning of the relationship process, not its end.

6. Give referrals whenever possible. The best networkers believe in the "givers gain" philosophy (what goes around comes around). If I help you, you will help me, and we will both do better due to it. In other words, if you do not genuinely attempt to help the people you meet, then you are not networking effectively. If you cannot give someone a bona fide referral, try to offer some information that might be of interest to them (such as details about an upcoming event).

7. Exchange business cards. Ask each person you meet for two cards-one to pass on to someone else and one to keep.

8. Manage your time efficiently. Spend 10 minutes or less with each person you meet, and do not linger with friends or associates. If your goal is to network with 15 to 20 people, be careful not to spend too much time with one person. When you meet someone interesting with whom you would like to speak further, set up an appointment for a later date.

9. Write notes on the backs of the business cards you collect. Record anything you think may be useful in remembering each person more clearly. Having notes on the people will come in handy when you follow up.

10. Follow up! Drop a note or give a call to each person you have met. Be sure to fulfill any promises you have made.

L.   Professional Appearance

If you look good, then you feel good. If you feel good, then you work great. Always remember that the first impression is everything. Professional dress is necessary for those who want to excel. It is vital for males and females in certain professions to obey the following rules and cheat sheets:

- **No visible tattoos; attempt to cover as many as possible**
- **No visible body art**
- **Well-groomed hair**
- **Well-groomed facial hair**
- **Well-tailored suit; in some industries, sport coats**
- **Well-polished dress shoes**
- **Wear a quality watch**
- **Pressed and adequately fitted clothes**
- **Since you are always networking, never leave home without looking crisp and professional**

In the following pages I will provide diagrams that will explain the different types of dress codes and what is considered to be acceptable dress for the intended occasion. As a rule, you never want to be underdressed or over dressed for an event, so use these are a reference when you are picking out an outfit.

*In the diagrams, all of the outfits that are associated with women are skirts and dresses. It is appropriate for women to wear pants.

UNACCEPTABLE

Men and women should avoid certain clothing in work settings unless explicitly told such clothing is acceptable.

MEN
Caps
Anything with holes
Sleeveless shirts
Open-toed or sock-less shoes
Shorts
Most Jewelry, aside from wrist or pocket watches

WOMEN
Caps
Anything with holes
Sleeveless shirts
Open-toed or sock-less shoes
Mini-skirts
Leggings with no accompanying legwear

ULTRA-CASUAL

Ultra-casual dress is a sweeping trend that allows employees to dress comfortably at work. But that doesn't mean you can wear your pajamas!

MEN
T-shirt
Collared or hooded sweater
Jeans
Comfortable footwear
Watch optional

WOMEN
T-shirt or fitted blouse
Collared or hooded sweater
Comfortable pants
Comfortable footwear
Jewelry optional

WHERE YOU'LL SEE THIS DRESS CODE
- Startups
- Tech firms
- "Millenial-friendly" workplaces
- Happy hours

NOTES
- Despite being "laid back", ultra-casual clothing shouldn't have holes or tears.
- Hats, shorts, leggings and open-toed shoes are often acceptable.

CASUAL

Casual dress allows you to be comfortable while still maintaining a somewhat professional appearance.

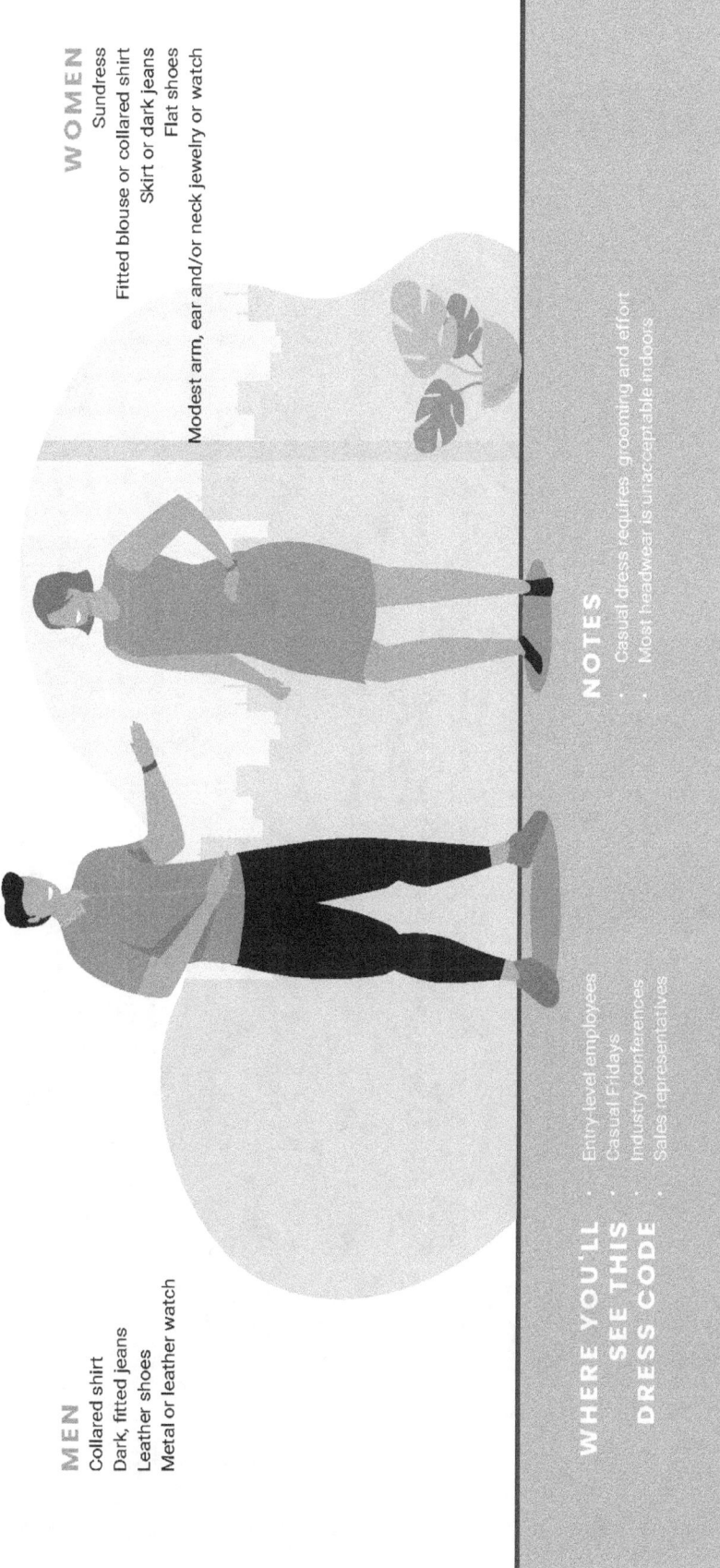

MEN
Collared shirt
Dark, fitted jeans
Leather shoes
Metal or leather watch

WOMEN
Sundress
Fitted blouse or collared shirt
Skirt or dark jeans
Flat shoes
Modest arm, ear and/or neck jewelry or watch

WHERE YOU'LL SEE THIS DRESS CODE
- Entry-level employees
- Casual Fridays
- Industry conferences
- Sales representatives

NOTES
- Casual dress requires grooming and effort
- Most headwear is unacceptable indoors

BUSINESS CASUAL

Business casual is typically the minimum dress code thoughout established or "traditional" business.

MEN
Blazer, sport coat, or sweater
Oxford or polo shirt
Dress pants
Leather shoes
Metal or fine leather watch

WOMEN
Fitted blouse or button-down shirt
Knee-length skirt or dress
Flats, sling-backs or boots
Watch or simple jewelry

WHERE YOU'LL SEE THIS DRESS CODE
- Entry-level employees at traditional companies
- Department managers
- Employer-sponsored events
- Internal and/or client-facing meetings

NOTES
- Business casual often uses solid, neutral colors and simple patterns

BUSINESS FORMAL

Business formal dress is the pinnacle of corporate attire and often distinguishes those in executive positions.

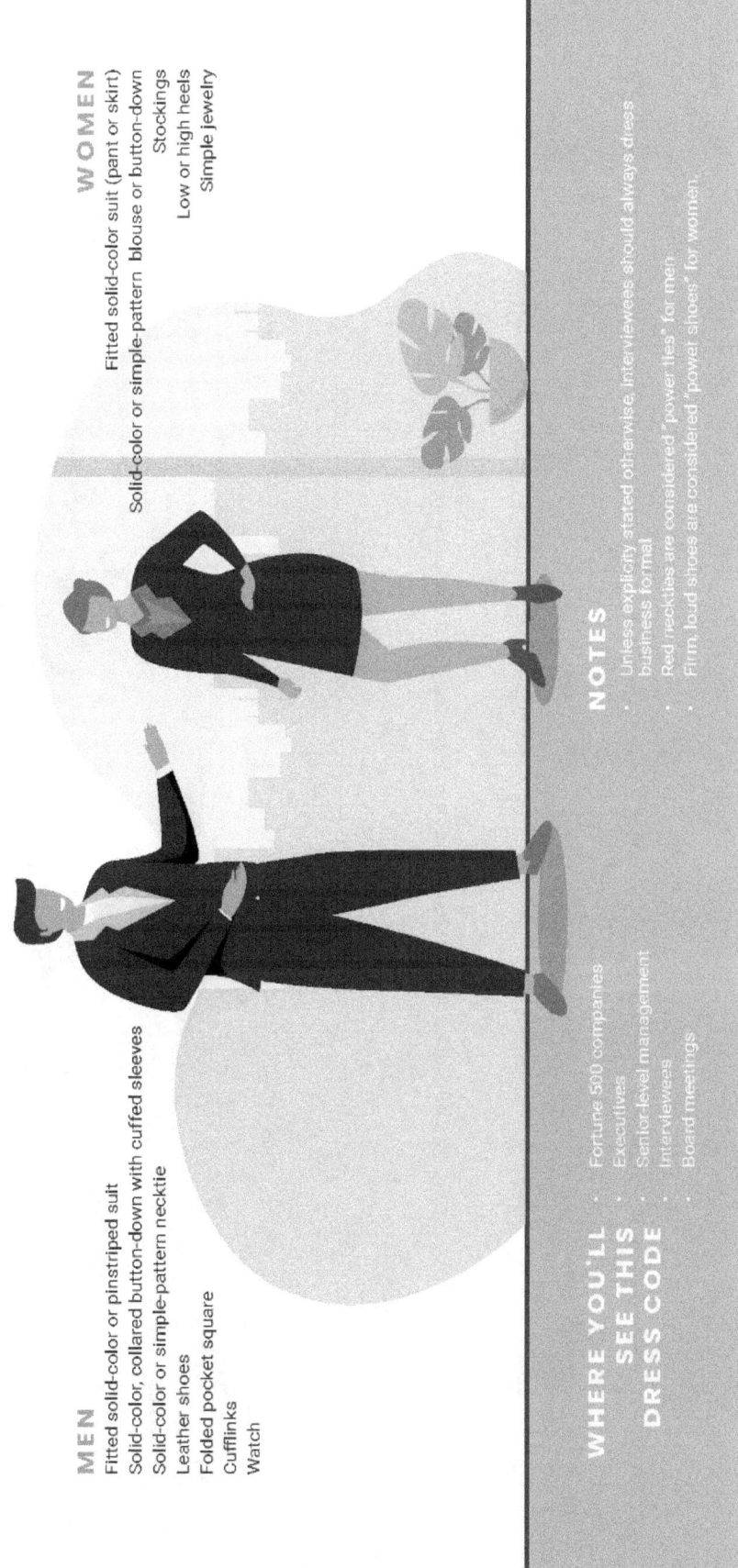

MEN

- Fitted solid-color or pinstriped suit
- Solid-color, collared button-down with cuffed sleeves
- Solid-color or simple-pattern necktie
- Leather shoes
- Folded pocket square
- Cufflinks
- Watch

WOMEN

- Fitted solid-color suit (pant or skirt)
- Solid-color or simple-pattern blouse or button-down
- Stockings
- Low or high heels
- Simple jewelry

WHERE YOU'LL SEE THIS DRESS CODE

- Fortune 500 companies
- Executives
- Senior-level management
- Interviewees
- Board meetings

NOTES

- Unless explicitly stated otherwise, interviewees should always dress business formal.
- Red neckties are considered "power ties" for men
- Firm loud shoes are considered "power shoes" for women.

SEMI-FORMAL

Semi-formal attire is frequently used for high-class social occasions like galas.

MEN
Dark three-piece suit
Neck or bow tie
Appropiate leather shoes
Collared shirt with cuffed sleeves
Metal watch

WOMEN
Cocktail dress or dress skirt and top
Elegant neck jewelry
Elegant or modest arm jewelry

WHERE YOU'LL SEE THIS DRESS CODE
- Galas
- Weddings

NOTES
- Despite its name, semi-formal is one of the most rigid forms of dress
- Semi-formal is often confused for the same style as "business formal"
- Semi-formal is considered over-the-top for a work day.

BLACK TIE

Black tie dress is reserved for significant occasions that require elegance, etiquette, and proper decorum.

MEN
Black tuxedo
Black bow tie
Black leather shoes
Solid white, collared shirt with cuffed sleeves
Metal watch

WOMEN
Full-length evening gown
Elegant neck jewelry
Elegant or modest arm jewelry

WHERE YOU'LL SEE THIS DRESS CODE
- Galas
- Major non-profit or political fundraisers

NOTES
- Black tie and semi-formal are often used interchangeably, but there are subtle differences.
- Black tie requires clothing most attendees do not have and may rent.
- Black tie is considered over-the-top for a work day.

FORMAL / WHITE TIE

Formal dress is often confused with simple suits and ties. In reality, it requires fine, uncommon garments that most people typically don't own - or can't afford.

MEN
- Black tuxedo
- Tailcoat
- Solid-color vest
- Solid-color shirt with collar and cuffs
- Lapel corsage
- Folded pocket square
- Wrist-length white or black gloves
- White bowtie
- Top hat, cane and/or overcoat.

WOMEN
- Full-length evening gown
- Elegant neck jewelry
- Full-length, solid-color gloves
- Elegand, heeled shoes
- Elegant, shawl, scarf, or overcoat (optional)

WHERE YOU'LL SEE THIS DRESS CODE
- Political or diplomatic events
- Executive corporate social events
- Anything labeled "high society"

NOTES
- Invitations to white tie events are indications of high social status
- Most people will never attend a white tie event
- Formal dress is never seen in the workplace

M. Table Etiquette

Having a meeting with a meal is a Hustle Culture weapon. One meeting with food is more valuable than any other gathering that you can possibly have. Food allows for more organic conversations. **I Want You to Learn Dine Like A Boss!** Dinner meetings aim to maintain your network, connect with critical players, and share your vision.

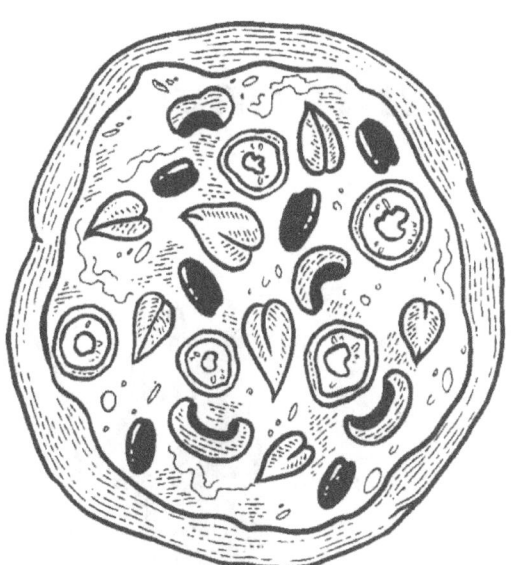

Conversation over food allows for you to explain your Hustle more naturally and authentically. However, how you present yourself while having dinner with a client or a supervisor can be an asset, hindrance, or a nightmare to your Hustle.

It may seem trivial, but table etiquette can maximize the impression you make by adding a dimension of confidence, professionalism, and class. A great meal is a way to separate your daily Hustle to connect but, most notably, showcase how cultured you are and how much of a Boss you are.

The best way to raise your game is to learn proper table settings for different occasions. I have included diagrams and samples of the major types of table settings.

1. Basic Table Setting

The picture above is an example of a basic table setting. This place setting is perfect when you are having an everyday meal or eating alone.

2. Informal Table Setting

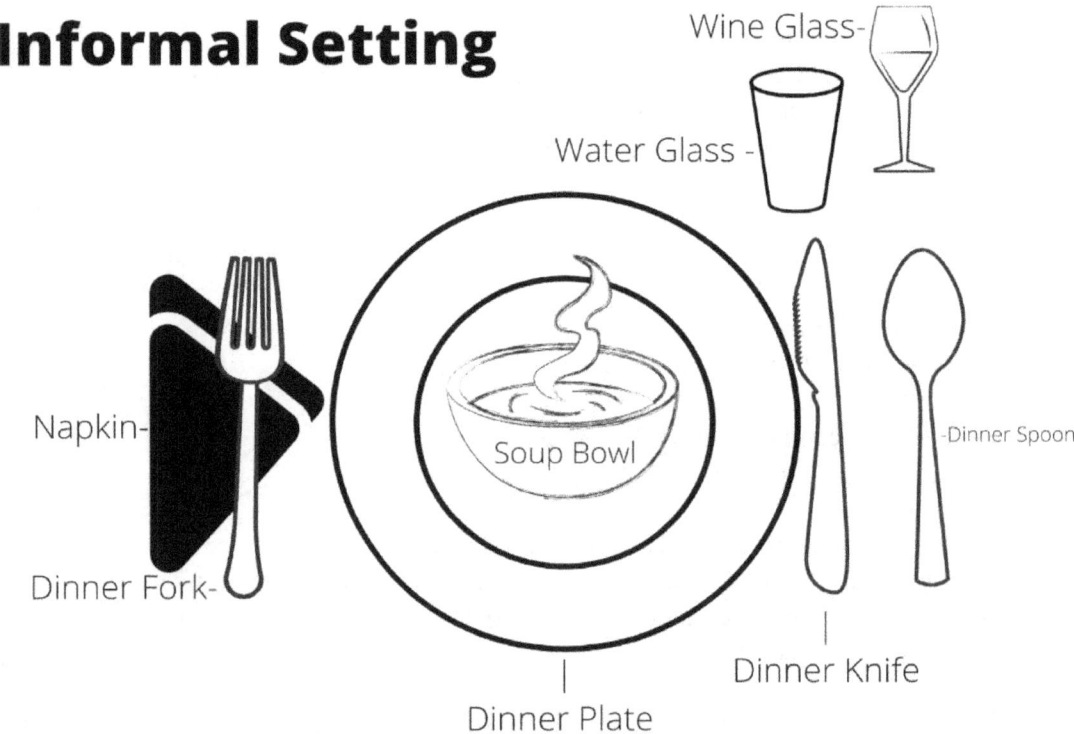

An informal table setting is a fantastic way to enjoy a meal with family or a casual dinner date. A relaxed, informal table setting is a basic table setting with a few minor adjustments.
- Decorate or Cloth Napkin-Under fork
- Soup Spoon
- Wine glass or other stemless glassware.

3. Formal Table Setting

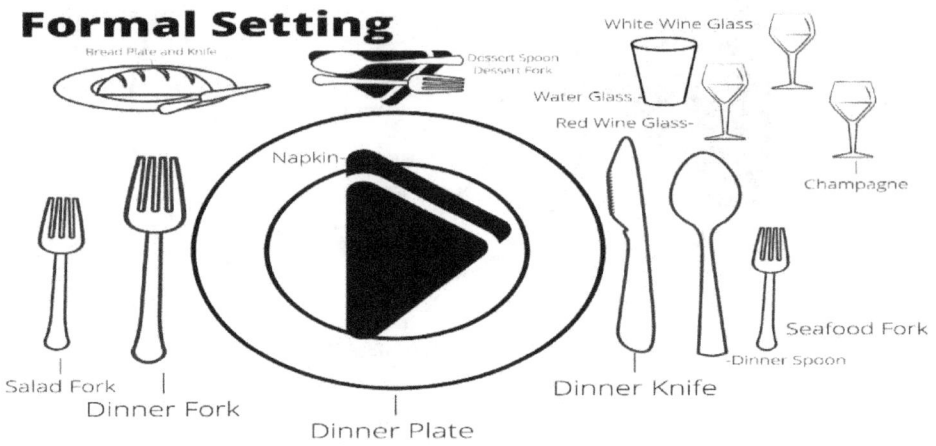

Formal Table Setting is for extravagant dinner parties or holidays. A formal traditional table setting is a perfect opportunity to showcase your dining "A" game. You start with an informal table setting above and then:

- You add a tablecloth or table runner.
- Place candles and flowers in the center of the table.
- Add cloth napkins, that is folded and put across the center of the dinner plate
- If you have valuable dishes (China) and high-quality silver flatware, this is the time to pull them out.
- Add a bread plate and small butter knife.
- If you have a salad, put a plate to the forks' direct left (Not Pictured).
- Place a dessert fork and spoon above the plate.
- If you are having steak, please put a steak knife to the right of the plate.
- Use stemmed wine glasses.
- If you possess charger plates (Large decorative plates), place them under the dinner plate.

4. Multi-Course Table Setting

A real Boss move is the multi-course meal table setting. Multi-Course meals range from 5 to 12 different courses. Multi-course meals will typically consist of soup, salad, fish course, main course, and dessert. The table setting above is considered a 5-course meal because you are eating five different courses of food.

A multi-course meal starts with the formal place setting then adds an assortment of forks, spoons, and knives. To show style, add name cards to each of the place settings. Since we have covered the different dining place setting types, the next few pages will cover additional rules.

DINING LIKE A BOSS
USE THE SILVERWARE FARTHEST FROM YOUR PLATE FIRST.

HERE IS THE SILVERWARE AND DINNERWARE RULE
Eat to your left, drink to your right. Any food dish to the left is yours, and any glass to the right is yours. Work from the outside in, you will be fine.

AMERICAN STYLE
Knife in right hand, fork in left hand holding food. After a few bite-sized pieces of food are cut, place knife on edge of plate with blades facing in. Eat food by switching fork to right hand (unless you are left-handed). A left hand, arm or elbow on the table is bad manners.

CONTINENTAL / EUROPEAN STYLE
Knife in right hand, fork in left hand. Eat food with fork still in left hand. The difference is that you do not switch hands – you eat with your fork in your left hand, with the prongs curving downward. Both utensils are kept in your hands with the tines pointed down throughout the entire eating process. If you take a drink, you do not just put your knife down, you put both utensils down into the resting position: cross the fork over the knife. Any unused silverware is simply left on the table.

Your napkin should be placed in your lap as soon as you are seated

Salt and Pepper are always passed together

Once a utensil has been used, it should not touch the table again

Never put your elbows on the table

THE BREAD AND BUTTER KNIFE SHOULD NEVER TOUCH THE TABLE

MEAL COURSES

12 COURSE MEAL
A 12 course dinner menu includes an hors d'oeuvre, amuse-bouche, soup, appetizer, salad, fish, first main course, palate cleanser, second main course, cheese course, dessert, and mignardise.

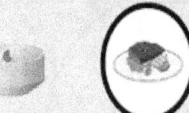

10 COURSE MEAL
A 10 course dinner menu includes an hors d'oeuvre, soup, appetizer, salad, fish, main course, palate cleanser, second main course, dessert, and mignardise.

9 COURSE MEAL
A 9 course dinner menu includes an hors d'oeuvre, soup, appetizer, salad, fish, main course, palate cleanser, dessert, and mignardise.

MAKING RESTAURANT RESERVATIONS:

Restaurant reservations are like any other appointment. If you make sure that you arrive on time. If you are going to be late more than 15 minutes call the restaurant to let them know your time of arrival or cancel.

8 COURSE MEAL
A An 8 course dinner menu includes an hors d'oeuvre, soup, appetizer, salad, main course, palate cleanser, dessert, and mignardise course dinner menu includes an hors d'oeuvre, amuse-bouche, soup, appetizer, salad, fish, first main course, palate cleanser, second main course, cheese course, dessert, and mignardise

7 COURSE MEAL
A 7 course dinner menu includes an hors d'oeuvre, soup, appetizer, salad, main course, dessert, and mignardise.

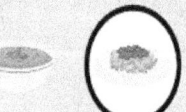

6 COURSE MEAL
A 6 course dinner menu includes an hors d'oeuvre, soup, appetizer, salad, main course, and dessert.

HOW TO USE NAPKINS:

IN A RESTAURANT
As soon as you are seated by the host or hostess, take the napkin from your place setting and unfold and place your napkin it on your lap. Unlike the movies it is not appropriate to fling the napkin open.

5 COURSE MEAL
A 5 course dinner menu includes an hors d'oeuvre, appetizer, salad, main course, and dessert.

4 COURSE MEAL
A 4 course dinner menu includes an hors d'oeuvre, appetizer, main course, and dessert.

3 COURSE MEAL
A 3 course dinner menu includes an appetizer, main course, and dessert.

- In some 5 star restaurants the waiter may place the napkin on your lap.
- The napkin is to remain on your lap during the entire meal.
- Never use the napkin to clean your silverware.
- Never wipe your face with your napkin
- Never use the napkin to wipe your nose.

If you have to leave the table this is called excusing yourself. Take the napkin fold it and place it on either side of the plate.
- Do not refold your napkins
- Do not wad your napkin on the table
- Do not leave napkin in your chair

At the end of the meal leave the napkin folded on the left side of the plate.

WHEN TO START EATING

IN A RESTAURANT: Wait until everyone in the dinner party has been served.

AT A PRIVATE DINNER PARTY: Please wait to your host or hostess pick up their fork and starts to eat. If the host or hostess tell you to start eating, then you may proceed.

AT A PRIVATE DINNER PARTY

If you are having a formal dinner at someone house. You are to unfold the napkin when the host or hostess unfold their napkin. At that time place your napkin on your lap and follow the uses as if you were at a restaurant.

At the end of the meal the hostess is supposed to place their napkin on the table. At the that point you are to place your napkin neatly folded to the left of the plate.

HOW TO USE YOUR SILVERWARE AND DINNERWARE

GENERAL SOCIAL AND DINING ETIQUETTE RULES

DRESS CODE
Follow whatever dress code is requested on the invitation or suggested by the host/hostess. Do your research on the restaurant before you go.

ARRIVAL
Always arrive 10 minutes early

HOSTESS GIFT
It is fitting to bring a small hostess gift, one that the hostess is not compelled to use that very evening.

SEATING
At a dinner party, wait for the host or hostess sits down before taking your seat. If the host/hostess asks you to sit, then do. "At a very formal dinner party, if there are no name cards at the table, wait until the host indicates where you should sit. The seating will typically be man-woman-man-woman with the women seated to the right of the men.

PRAYER
A prayer or 'blessing' may be customary in some households. The dinner guests may join in or be respectfully silent. Most prayers are made by the host before the meal is eaten.

TOAST
Sometimes a toast is offered instead of a prayer. Always join in with a toast. If the host stands up during the toast, also stand up.

END OF DINNER
Serving tea or coffee signifies that the formal part of the evening is over. Guests may now feel free to leave, or linger if the host or hostess encourages them to do so.

THANK YOU NOTE
After a formal dinner party, a thank you note should be sent to the hostess. Depending on how well you know your hosts, a telephone call is also acceptable.

SERVING FOOD
Food is served from the left. Dishes are removed from the right. Always say please when asking for something. At a restaurant, be sure to say thank you to your server and bus boy after they have removed any used items. Butter, spreads, or dips should be transferred from the serving dish to your plate before spreading or eating.

PASSING DISHES OR FOOD
Pass food from the left to the right. Do not stretch across the table, crossing other guests, to reach food or condiments.

EATING
DO NOT TALK WITH FOOD IN YOUR MOUTH!
Always taste your food before seasoning it
IT IS VERY RUDE TO ADD SALT AND PEPPER BEFORE TASTING THE FOOD.
- Do not blow on your food to cool it off
- Always scoop food, using the proper utensil, away from you
- Eat in small bites and slowly
- Do eat a little of everything on your plate
- Even if you have dietary restrictions, let your host know in advance of the dinner
- Do not "play with" your food or utensils
- Never wave or point silverware
- Keep elbows off the table
- Do not talk with your mouth full
- Chew with your mouth closed
- Do not talk excessively loud
- Loud eating noises such as slurping and burping are very impolite
- Turn off your cell phone or switch it to silent
- Leave plates and glasses where they are don stack

PROPER TIPPING ETIQUETTE IN A RESTAURANT

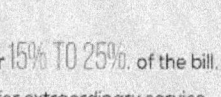

At a restaurant, always leave a tip. Tips can vary from 15% TO 25%.

| Waiter 15% TO 25%. of the bill. 25%. for extraordinary service | Waiter 15% TO 20%. of the bill. 25%. |

| Wine steward 15% of wine bill. | Bartender 10% TO 15%. of bar bill. |

| Coat Check $1.00 per coat | Car attendant $2.00 TO $5.00 |

Pre- Meal Rules
1. Eat Something ahead of time.
2. Dress Professionally
3. Silence your device
4. Arrive Early

Introduction Rules

1. If you are a male, you should always rise when introducing or being introduced to someone.
2. Provide information when making an introduction "Ken, please meet K.A. Perkins, CEO of G & P Unlimited Co, Inc."
3. Unless given permission, always address someone by his or her title and last name (Mr., Ms., Mrs., Dr., etc.,).
4. Practice a firm handshake. Make eye contact while shaking hands.

During Meal

When you have your meal, please observe the following rules:

1. Wait to sit until the host/hostess indicates the seating arrangement.
2. Place Materials under your seat.
3. Never order the most expensive item.
4. Place the napkin in the lap before eating or drinking anything.
5. When ordering, keep in mind that this is a *talking* business meal. Order something easy to eat, such as boneless chicken or fish.
6. Avoid Trouble Food- Sauces, Spaghetti, Hamburgers, and Finger Foods.
7. Do not hold the order up because you cannot decide. Feel free to ask for suggestions from others at the table.
8. Wait to eat until everyone has been served.
9. Keep hands in your lap unless you are using them to eat.
10. Practice proper posture; sit up straight with your arms close to your body.
11. Bring food to your mouth—not your head to the plate.
12. Try to eat at the same pace as everyone else.
13. Take responsibility for keeping up the conversation.
14. Place the napkin on the chair seat if excusing yourself for any reason.
15. Place a napkin beside the plate at the end of the meal.
16. Push the chair under the table when excusing yourself.

When Eating and Drinking

1. Never order alcoholic beverages (21+)
    1. Club Soda with lemon is ideal. Club soda is sign that in another setting, you would drink.
    2. Iced Tea or lemonade is another option.
    3. If they suggest a drink, only order one, either beer or wine. Never order spirits (Whiskey, Rum, Vodka, Tequila, Bourbon, etc.,)!
    4. Always drink slower than the host.
2. Start eating with the silverware that is farthest away from your plate.

1. You may have two spoons and two forks. The spoon farthest away from your plate is a soup spoon.
2. The fork farthest away is a salad fork unless you have three forks, one being much smaller, which would be a seafood fork for an appetizer.
3. The dessert fork/spoon is usually above the plate. Remember to work from the outside in

3. Dip soup away from you; sip from the side of the spoon.
4. Season food only after you have tasted it.
    1. Pass salt and pepper together—even if asked for only one.
5. Pass all items to the right.
    1. If the item has a handle, such as a pitcher, pass with the handle toward the next person.
    2. For bowls with spoons, pass with the spoon, ready for the next person.
    3. If you are the one to reach to the center of the table for an item, pass it before serving yourself.
6. While you are speaking during a meal, utensils should be resting on the plate (fork and knife crossed on the plate with tines down).
7. Do not chew with your mouth open or blow on your food.

Post Meal

1. Always make a move to pay even when you were not expected to pay (carry money and only order what you can pay for).
2. Always remember to thank the host.

N. Honesty/Ethics/Integrity

Most employers will place honesty at the top of the employment must-haves. Honest people are trusted, people. If an employer depends on you, they will value you, which equates to raises and promotions. Honesty is also important when you are dealing with coworkers and customers. A customer will never return, and a coworker will always be leery of you if you have been dishonest with them.

Integrity is a lifestyle of honesty and morality. It is the inward code that you live by. Integrity operates not only when you work, but when you are off the clock, when no one is watching. These are ten examples of personal integrity:

- Taking responsibility for your actions.
- Choosing to do the right thing when no one is watching.

- Putting the needs of others above your own.
- Offering to help others in need.
- Giving others the benefit of the doubt and a chance to explain.
- Choosing to be honest in all things, even if it means personal repercussions.
- Showing respect to everyone, regardless of their title or position.
- Having a balance between confidence and being arrogant.
- Being able to admit that you were wrong to anyone.
- Being a person that is committed to follow-through.
- Living your life with a sense of loyalty.

O. Flexibility/Adaptability

Can you adapt? If you can, then you will thrive in the workforce. Things will happen, regardless of your chosen industry, that will disrupt your day. Nevertheless, you still must accommodate those disruptions. Therefore, you must have a daily attack plan (See the section on Organization and Time Management). Inconvenience is not fun and can be quite frustrating. However, successful people can adjust and still get everything done. The Hustle requires you to accommodate your customers, company, and family.

P. Independence/Self-Motivation/Initiative

You must be a self-starter. You must produce with little or no supervision. You must be self-motivated to take the initiative and get things done. While others are doing what is required, your Hustle will grab people's attention and give you a Hustle Culture advantage.

Q. Reliability/Responsibility

People, employers, and customers expect that you will be at work each day, on time, and prepared to work. This shows you are dependable and mindful. No organization can function with a representative that frequently arrives late with a variety of excuses. Be reliable, own up to what you do, be responsible, and never place the fault elsewhere. If you have a habit of being late, then work on. Your time management and organization.

R. Leadership

Leadership is your ability to leverage other's strengths to achieve common goals. As you display interpersonal skills, your capacity to coach and develop others increases. When you show leadership, others will follow because you have the ability to guide and motivate teams to advance your organizational outcomes, which enhances your Hustle.

S. Professionalism

Being professional is your ability to exhibit responsibility and successful work propensities (e.g., dependability, punctuality, teamwork, time management, and organization skills) while demonstrating integrity and ethical behavior.

T. Career Management

Career management is your ability to distinguish and identify your aptitudes, qualities, knowledge, and experience pertinent to your mission and vision. If you are adept at career management, you can recognize personal and professional growth opportunities while making strides to enhance your career.

U. Global/Intercultural Fluency

Global and Intercultural Fluency means that you have an appreciation, value, and regard for different communities, races, ages, sexes, sexual preferences, and religious beliefs. It is a skill to connect with people who are different from you.

3. Verbal Communication

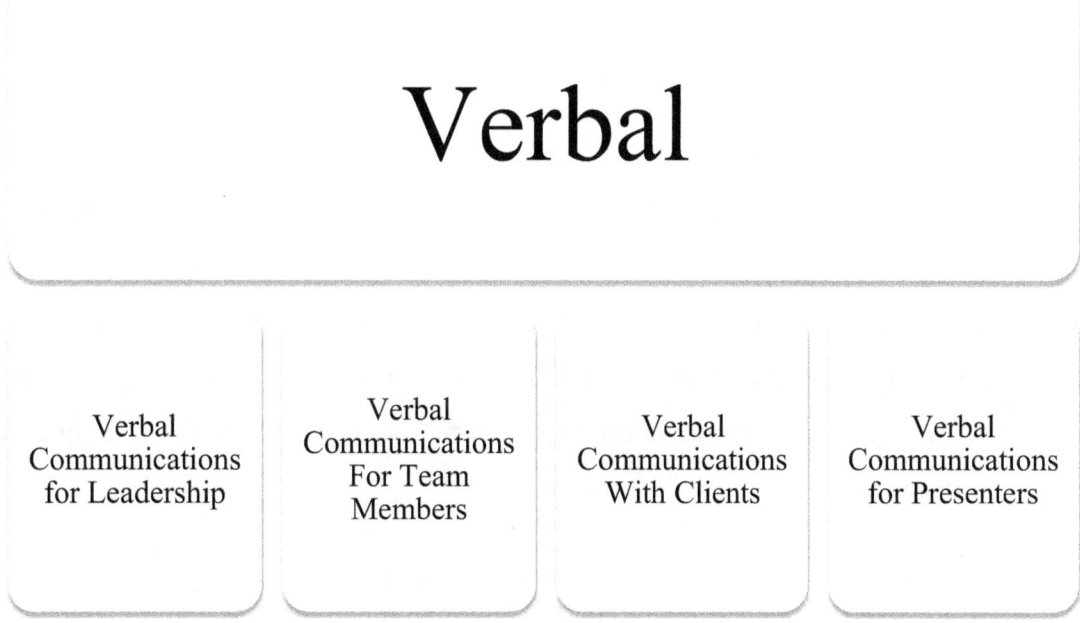

Every industry requires some level of verbal communication. Verbal communication can be in the form of presentations, sales, and customer service. The Verbal Communication section will give you the skills to enhance your communication skills, regardless of whether you are a leader, team member, sales/customer service representative, and/or a corporate presenter.

Verbal Communications for Leadership: When you are in leadership, it is essential to concentrate and give your employees or team members your undivided attention. You need to comprehend their needs, points of view, and give them chances to elevate and encourage them. The following is a list of communication tools you must use as a leader:

- Decisiveness with stakeholders
- Guiding employees regarding appropriate course of action
- Correcting employees in an effective and timely manner.
- Giving credit to those who deserve it
- Recognizing and addressing staff dissatisfaction
- Speaking clearly and in control at all times
- Training others to complete their responsibilities efficiently
- Connecting with your staff
- Supporting and sharing with team members
- Modeling the corporate mission, vision, and strategic plan

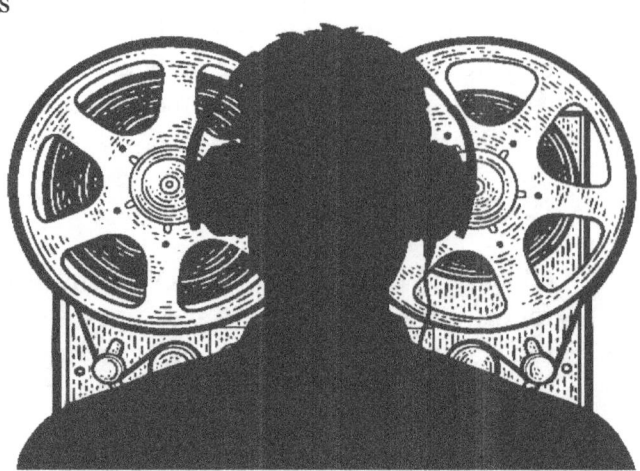

Verbal Communications with Customers: Everything that we do as professionals revolves around customers. The goal of any industry is to create capital and profit for the organization. Regardless of whether you are providing a product or service, you must have effective verbal communication with the client and/or customer. Effective verbal communication with customers should be focused on the customers' needs. The following is a list of communication tools you must use if you are in sales or customer service:

- Foreseeing the concerns of your customers
- Questioning customers for clarification
- De-escalating clients while responding to their dissatisfaction
- Clearly explaining to the customers, the advantages of product or service

Verbal Communications for Team Members: If you are on a team, your communication must be open and focused on facilitating group achievement. The following is a list of communication skills that you must have when you are working on a team:

- Encouraging collaboration among team members
- Explaining job conflicts and circumstances while working to find collaborative solutions
- Proactively soliciting help from team members
- Asking questions to inspire more insight concerning work-related issues
- Being able to receive and give meaningful feedback
- Stating your needs without criticizing and blaming leadership or team members

Verbal Communications for Presenters: Public speaking is a needed skill, and it will give you leverage in any industry. When you have mastered verbal communication as a presenter, you have a strategic advantage because most people have a fear of public speaking. Effective communication to audiences includes:

- Appealing to your audience while introducing your subject
- Pronouncing each word, you speak
- Preparing your training before you deliver it
- Tell stories to show focus and connection to the stated subject
- Selecting language suitable to the crowd (Culture, Context, and Concepts)
- Speaking with enthusiasm and confidence

4. **Written Communication**

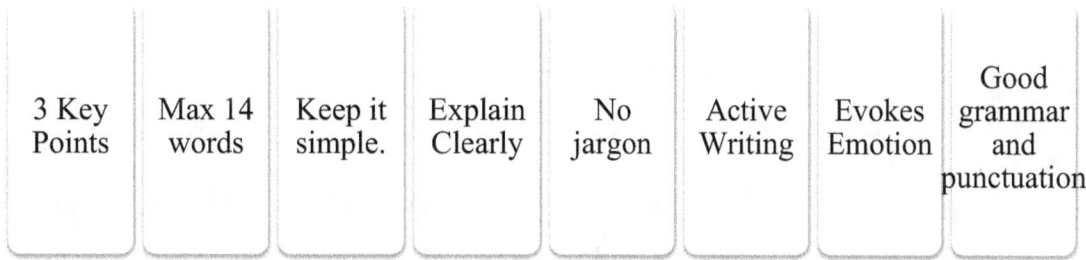

Written communication is vital because the more you are involved in leadership, the more you are engaged in writing. All correspondence must be free of spelling and grammatical errors. Using spell check is essential, but it will not catch the wrong word usage. Many employees have lost jobs due to poor writing. Incorporate these tips:

- Writing should have no more than 3 Key Points.
- Sentences should be no longer than 14 words. Less is always more.
- Refrain from using overly complicated words. Keep it simple.
- Explain what you want the reader to do.

- Refrain from using jargon.
- Use Active vs. Passive writing; it will strengthen your message.
- Make sure your writing evokes emotion.
- Good grammar and punctuation are essential.

*Note: If you struggle with writing, I suggest using online tools such as Grammarly, Outwrite, or Wordtune to assist with grammar and spelling.

5. Teamwork

Communication	Management	Listening	Reliability	Respectfulness
Advising	Cooperation	Active Listening	Commitment	Acknowledging Others
Collaboration	Critical Thinking	Ask Clarifying Questions	Community Building	Encouragement
Contributing	Defining Problems	Attentive	Confidence	Expanding Ideas
Coordination	Empathy	Eye Contact	Confidence Building	Interpersonal Motivation
Creativity	Flexibility	Give Feedback	Dependability	Opinion Exchange
Creative Thinking	Emotional Intelligence	Group Decision Making	Flexibility	Patience
Give Feedback	Leadership	Hearing Concerns	Helpfulness	Positive Attitude
Goal Setting	Listening	Interpreting Nonverbal Communication	Honesty	Relationship Building
Guidance	Logic	Open Mind	Participation	Sharing Credit
Influencing	Logical Argument	Patience	Perform Tasks	Support
Persuading	Logical Thinking	Relaxed	Responsibility	Team Player
Research	Mediation	Receive Feedback	Team Oriented	Tact
Management	Negotiating	Summarize	Task Management	Understanding Feelings
Teaching	Problem Solving		Trust	
Verbal Communication	Team Building			
Visual Communication				
Written Communication				

Teamwork is vitally necessary to serve as a leader and as a member of a group. It is imperative that you have the skills to work with groups of people to accomplish a goal or an objective. The chart above shows how you can effectively contribute to a team through communication, management, listening, reliability, and respectfulness.

6. Leadership Skills

Leadership is one of the essential tools that you need to be successful. Every individual is a leader; accordingly, you must learn what skills are required to lead people and organizations. As a leader, you must develop the art of inspiring and motivating people to reach higher levels of potential. This is important because it is through leadership that individuals, companies, communities, and governments can be transformed. It is only through leadership that ideas become products, and products can become business. Leadership is the foundation to change the world that we live in. The following is a list of leadership styles and the famous leaders that used them:

Leadership Style	Summary	Famous Example
Transactional Leadership	A transactional leader establishes a clear chain of command using an award and punishment method of managing activities.	Joseph McCarthy Charles de Gaulle Bill Gates
Transformational Leadership	A transformational leader is a leader that inspires staff by creating a workplace atmosphere of stimulation through the process of encouragement, inspiration, and innovation.	Martin Luther King, Jr. Walt Disney. Indra Nooyi Jacinda Ardern Oprah Winfrey Michelle Obama Carly" Fiorina
Servant Leadership	A servant leader is a leader that encourages collective decision and intelligent decision making. This type of leadership style puts the needs of the employees first.	George Washington Gandhi Cesar Chavez Hilary Clinton
Autocratic Leadership	An autocratic leader is a leader that has substantial power on staff, rarely deems worker recommendations, or give out control. This type of leader usually leads centered on their ideas.	Genghis Khan. King Henry VIII. Queen Elizabeth I. Napoleon Bonaparte. Father Junipero Serra. Queen Isabella I. Margaret Thatcher Angela Merkel Donald Trump
Laissez-faire Leadership	A laissez-faire leadership is a leader that has hands-off leadership approach. This leadership style is rooted in the leader's ability to trust their team. They allow their team members to use their creativity and gifts to meet identified goals.	Herbert Hoover Andrew Mellon Martin Van Buren Queen Victoria Warren Buffet George W. Rush Jr.
Democratic/Participative Leadership	A democratic leader is a a leader by which team members take a more proactive role in the decision-making process this type of	Jim Lentz Richard Branson Bob Diamond Jack Stahl James Parker

	leadership style is designed to include for all stakeholders' input before making a final decision.	
Bureaucratic Leadership	A bureaucratic leader is a leader whereby team members are made to follow specific rules and lines of authority created by the superiors with strict adherence.	Steve Easterbrook Harold Genene Alfred P Sloan Shinji Sogō Winston Churchill Nancy Pelosi
Charismatic Leadership	A charismatic leader is a leader that has a uniquely skill to communicate. In the case of a charismatic leader case, the leader manages people through a high aptitude for verbal and interpersonal connection. This type of leader can sell the mission and vision of the organization at a deep and emotional level.	Barack Obama Satya Nadella Bernadette Devlin Manny Pacquiao Rihanna Bono Aung San Suu Kyi George Clooney Ai Weiwei
Situational Leadership	A situational leader is an adaptive leader. Situational leadership uses a rage of the leadership model in certain situations to reach the desired outcome.	Dwight Eisenhower George Patton. Pat Summit Colin Powell. Phil Jackson Condoleezza Rice

7. Research Skills

Every industry is designed to solve a problem or to enhance the lives of people. Having research skills will empower you to identify an issue and gather the information that can help address the issue. Having this skill will make you more of an asset to your organization, whether you are an employer or an employee. It is critical to have the ability to gather information from various sources to develop the best methods for conducting business. This will give you a competitive Hustle Culture advantage. Effective research includes the use of the internet, library, and trade publications and journals.

8. Assimilating Data

Assimilating Data is the ability to use numbers, graphs, and charts to formulate logical business outcomes or forecasts. Every industry is driven by numbers and the interpretation of those numbers. This can include profits, production, and or outcomes.

Having the ability to conduct surveys and perform needs analysis will make you a commodity and set you apart.

9. Data Interpretation

Data Interpretation is the execution of strategies through which information is reviewed to arrive at an informed conclusion. A skilled data interpreter can take and process information and formulate a decision about the information. If you can use data to implement systems and solutions, you and your company have increased value.

10. Problem Solving

Regardless of whether you are an employee, employer, or entrepreneur, it is important for individuals to research, gather data, and interpret data. Once that information has been interpreted, it must be used to solve problems. Problem-solving increases your workplace value. To be an effective problem solver, you must be able to do four things:

1. *Focus on the solution, not the problems.*
2. *Develop a list of possible solutions to the problem.*
3. *Think of innovative ways to arrive at a solution.*
4. *Make your solution simple.*

Pillar 2-Hustle Culture Competencies

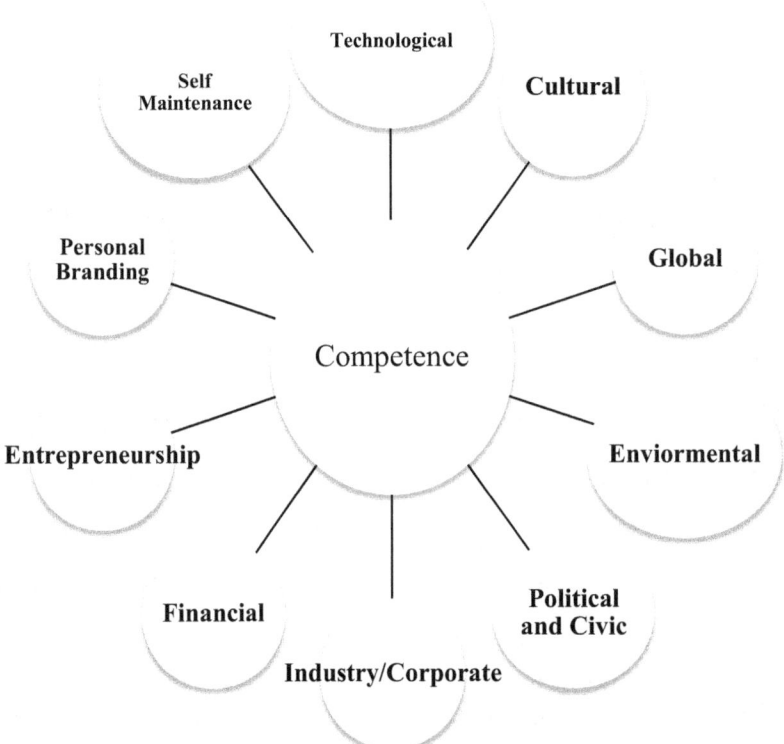

Developing, executing, and integrating a Hustle Culture Lifestyle can be awe-inspiring. There is a ton of material in this manual for you to learn. Remember, Hustle Culture is a way of life, not a program. Granted, some folks will transition and evolve immediately; for others, it will take time. It took me twenty years, and I am still discovering, learning, and sharping my skills! The key to enhancing your Hustle Cultural Skills is directly connected to developing your Hustle Cultural Competencies.

A Hustle Culture Competency is the knowledge, abilities and behaviors that contribute to an individual's capacity to perform well in the workforce environment. Hustle Culture Competencies that will help you move towards your purpose and vision for your life. It is through a set of well-defined Hustle Culture Competencies that you will be able to manage your success. In this section, you will find that some of the Hustle Culture Competencies come naturally, while other competencies will need to be learned and practiced.

1. Technological Competence

The world is an international community. You must understand how to utilize technology. Technological competence includes not only computers but also industry-standard software. You must use cell phones, tablets, smart phones, GPS, LCD Projectors, 3D Printers, virtual reality and etc. It is critical that you understand and have a working knowledge of technological innovation and its ability to impact the world and the global economy; and more importantly, use it to leverage your time.

The ability to leverage existing technologies ethically and efficiently to solve problems, complete tasks, and accomplish goals will give you a competitive advantage. The following chart is the comprehensive list of essential workforce-related technological competencies. The goal is to have a basic understanding of technology's use and function for general business applications.

Technological Competence		
Competence	**Definition**	**Example**
Operation Systems Navigation	The operating system is the software that is used to allow the computer to function. Operation systems have the same purpose, but each contains unique functions and sometimes different software.	Windows, macOS, Linux, Chrome
Spreadsheets Competence	Spreadsheet competence is the ability to use software to organize, calculate, graph, and analyze data.	Excel, Numbers, Sheets, Calc, Microsoft Certifications
Website Competence	Website competence is the ability to create simple websites for business and personal branding.	Wix, Shopify, Squarespace, WordPress
Email Competence	Email competence is the ability to use email in a professional setting.	See Section on Email Etiquette. (Pillar 1)
File Competence	File Competence is a fundamental technique for naming, storing, and handling documents.	N/A
Electronic Banking Competence	Electronic banking competence is the ability to make electronic transactions through mobile banking systems. These transactions consist of obtaining account balances, history, bill pay, remote check deposits, p2p payments, and finances transfers between a consumer's or any other accounts.	-All Banks -PayPal -Cashapp -Square-up -Crypto App
Digital Content Competence	Digital Content Competence is the ability to create graphics, take and edit photos and videos for website and social media postings.	Adobe Spark Canvas Photoshop Illustrator
Customer Relationship Management Competence	Customer Relationship Management (CRM) Competence is the use of technology for managing all your organization's relationships and interactions with customers and clients.	Salesforce Zoho

Cloud-Based Competence	Cloud-Based Competence is the ability to use applications, retrieve files, and collaborate with others through cloud computing servers.	Dropbox Google Drive Sharepoint OneDrive iCloud
Ecommerce Competence	Ecommerce Competence is the ability to set-up and conduct transactions through the internet and mobile devices.	See Mobile Banking See Website
Video Conferencing Competence	Video Conferencing Competence is the ability to set-up, host, and participate in video conferencing.	Zoom Ring central Microsoft Teams Skype Hangout Free Conference Call Google Meets
Computer Storage Devices Competence	Computer Storage Devices Competence is the ability to transfer files from a computer to other devices using storage devices.	Thumb drives Portable HD CD's DVDs" s
Cell Phones Competency	Cell Phones Competency is the use of cellphone for business uses.	
Social Media Competency	Social Media Competency is the ability to use multiple social media platforms for marketing, sales, and brand awareness.	Facebook Twitter Instagram Tumblr LinkedIn
Electronic Presentation Competency	Electronic Presentation Competencies the ability to create mixed media slideshow presentations.	PowerPoint Slides Keynote Microsoft Certifications
Desktop Publishing Competency	Desktop Publishing Competency is the ability to create word documents and create newsletters, signs, banners, and posters.	Word Publisher Doc Pages Microsoft Certifications

2. Cultural Competence

Cultural Competence is the understanding and appreciation for diversity. Through immigration and technology, the world is becoming smaller. Unlike previous generations you have the ability connect with others who are different from yourself. This global connectedness requires that you become more considerate of other people's cultural norms and beliefs. Cultural Competence is having the willingness to learn about various cultures from individuals' manners, customs, dress, language, religion, and rituals. Here are ten things you can do to increase cultural competence:

1. Develop and implement training and coaching in cultural competence in your organization and/or attend workshops presented outside of your organization.
2. Develop communication and relationships among diverse cultures of people.
3. Practice active listening.
4. Be sensitive to individual language barriers.
5. Encourage sensitivity to issues like time, local customs, religious matters, and etiquette.
6. Be aware and promote cross-cultural team building.
7. Be intentional in interacting with people from other cultures.
8. Be aware and address cultural insensitivity and jokes.
9. Never participate in conversations that promote cultural, racial, and gender stereotypes.
10. Refrain from using language that appears to be culturally biased or culturally dismissive.

3. Global Competence

We are now living in a global economy; therefore, it is critical to be competent in global awareness. It is critical for you to understand international trade and international business. With a global economy, international events affect every nation's economy, not just that of the United States. The United States' economic sustainability is more complicated than in previous generations because it involves other countries. For this reason, you must not only be competitive on the National level, but you must make yourself competitive on International level. The best preparation for this is to become a 21st-century learner and problem solver. Here are some practices you can put in place to increase your global competence to make you are a global asset in your industry:

- Learn how to apply different perspectives to solve problems and make decisions.
- Demonstrate resilience in new situations.
- Learn how to formulate decisions and opinions based on research, exploration, and evidence.
- Own and commit to lifelong learning and reflection.
- Learn how to collaborate with others.
- Share expertise and encourage discourse.

- Approach thinking and problem-solving collaboratively.
- Have a willingness to participate in new opportunities, ideas, and methods of learning and thinking.
- Have the willingness to engage with others.
- Know who you are an what you contribute to the global economy.
- Learn how to value more than one perspective.
- Discover ways to be comfortable with ambiguity & unfamiliar conditions.
- Discover ways to be adaptable and cognitively nimble.
- Show empathy.
- Show humility.
- Listen actively.
- Be Technologically Competent.

4. Environmental Competence

Companies and customers are looking for individuals that have innovative ideas for the conservation of our natural resources. Therefore, it is critical that you have environmental competence. Every industry is transitioning from merely a cost-effective process to what is environmentally responsible. The global and national markets are looking for individuals and organizations willing to help the environment. You can do specific things to help set a foundation to develop your journey to environmental competence.

1. Switch to LEDs Lights or convert your house to a smart home
2. Make your home more energy efficient
3. Eat Sustainable Foods
4. Plant Trees
5. Keep your vehicle in tip-top shape
6. Donate unused items to /local charities.
7. Give up plastics
8. Donate food to the homeless
9. Conserve water
10. Take showers, not baths
11. Be car-conscious
12. Walk, bike, or take public transit
13. Reduce, Reuse, Recycle
14. Start composting
15. Turn off the lights
16. Grow your own food
17. Eat leftovers
18. Shop virtually
19. Bring your bag when you shop
20. Incorporate a vegetarian day into your weekly diet

5. Political and Civic Competence

Political and Civic Competence is vital to your understanding of national policies as it relates to domestic and foreign issues. It is also critical for you to understand the Democratic, Independent, and Republican political platforms. Having a firm understanding of presidential politics is essential. It is also necessary to participate and engage in state and local governmental issues. Your participation on these levels is beneficial because the local and state levels' decisions affect education, housing, economy, business, and social programs. I have included a chart to help you learn more about how you can engage in civic knowledge and how to engage in civic activism.

Political and Civic Competence		
Civic Knowledge	Civic Skills	Civic Activism
<ul><li>Efficiency, Equity, Social Justice</li><li>Inclusiveness, collaboration, building constituency</li><li>Civic institutions, business, community participation, public work</li><li>Political Party Platforms</li><li>Responsible citizenship</li><li>Human Rights</li><li>Political and legal processes</li><li>Historical review of policy</li><li>Current Affairs</li><li>Diversity/Pluralism</li><li>Globalization and interdependence</li><li>Multiplicity Citizenship</li><li>Cosmopolitan citizenship</li><li>Representative government</li><li>Accountable government</li><li>Freedom of speech</li><li>Equality before the law</li><li>Social justice</li><li>Environmental Justice</li></ul>	<ul><li>Critical reasoning about causes and morality</li><li>Democratic decision making</li><li>Social organizing</li><li>Coordinated interactions</li><li>Interactive participation</li><li>Active citizenship practices</li><li>Cooperation</li><li>Consensus-building</li><li>Policy formation and analysis</li><li>Assessing the feasibility of change from social action and commitment</li></ul>	<ul><li>Stay informed</li><li>Read and subscribe to daily newspapers</li><li>Carry a pocket-sized constitution</li><li>Get the facts on any politician or political candidate</li><li>Vote-Local, state, and national elections</li><li>Volunteer to register voters</li><li>Volunteer to work at a polling place</li><li>Offer to drive elderly voters or those without transportation to the polls</li><li>Communicate with your elected officials</li><li>Attend a city council or community board meeting</li><li>Join a political campaign</li><li>Get involved with the local school board.</li><li>Join a political party</li><li>Run for office</li><li>Identify a problem in your community and work with your neighbors to fix it.</li><li>Paint a mural in a</li></ul>

| | | - public space (with permission)
- Pick up trash in your or someone else's neighborhood
- Collect food for those in need
- Visit a nursing home or hospital
- Donate blood or plasma
- Take a first aid class
- Clean up the local park
- Shop local and support small businesses
- Volunteer
- Host or attend a debate watch party in your community
- Host a picnic or block party in your neighborhood |
|--|--|--|

6. Industry/Corporate Competence

Industry and Corporate Competence is understanding the language and the unwritten rules of your industry. Having an early grasp of what it takes to get a promotion and increase your value is based on the organization. Many individuals enter the workforce not knowing how to get to the next level. Industry and Corporate competence are vital because it provides a blueprint for what it takes to go from entry-level to management, and from management to executive.

7. Financial Competence

Financial Competence is an understanding of how money works. It is crucial that you understand banking, investing, and insurance. Financial Competence is also learning the value of credit and debt. I have provided a list of ten essential financial terms that you need to learn and study. I have included at the end of the manual a list of books that will help develop your Financial Competence.

Financial Competence

Credit Cards	Learn the basics of how credit cards work and how you can use them to your advantage while not using them when they are not to your advantage.
Compound Interest	Appreciate the full potential and power of investing. You need to understand how compound interest works and what it can do overtime to your investments.
Risk	Learn that risk is part of investing, and you can significantly increase your wealth by taking calculated financial risks.
Index Funds	It is a simple and cost-efficient way to get into the stock market. Index funds are a portfolio of stock and bonds that allows you to take full advantage of the compound interest discussed above without the major risks of investing in individual stocks. When you invest in index funds you are investing in multiple stock and bonds at the same time.
Housing and Mortgage	As the number of different mortgages become available to borrowers increases, you need to understand how these new mortgages work.
Depreciating Assets	Not everything you purchase is an investment; therefore, it is vital to understand the difference between an appreciating asset and a depreciating asset. Items people buy, like cars, will decrease in value over time. That does not mean that they are bad purchases to make, as it can be an essential factor in your overall earning potential. However, it does mean you should be purchasing these at the best price you can and not buying more than you need.
Emergency Fund	Life will always throw unexpected curves into even the best-laid plans. Being prepared with an emergency fund is an essential part of your financial literacy. Unexpected financial losses will occur but having an available resource for these emergencies can be the difference between remaining financially healthy and finding yourself financially struggling.
Taxes	Although they can seem completely overwhelming and incomprehensible, it is essential for you to understand the basics of how taxes work.
Budget	There is not anything more important than knowing where the money you earn is going. Calculate your expenses and make a budget.
Cryptocurrency	A cryptocurrency is a digital asset designed to work as a new medium of exchange. Cryptocurrencies use decentralized control as opposed to centralized digital currency and central banking system. Cryptocurrency is now becoming a global form of currency and a medium of exchange. Therefore, it is crucial that you learn how to use this currency as a means of exchange.

8. Entrepreneurship Competence

America is a capitalist country. The foundation of this nation is rooted in business. It is essential for you to understand that you are in a rapidly changing economy and you can no longer think that you will work for one company for thirty years then retire. You must develop a level of entrepreneurship or business ownership. It is imperative to create multiple streams of income, and in many cases, that includes owning your own business. Entrepreneurship is like financial literacy. I will provide a list of books and resources at the end of the book for you to use to expand your entrepreneurship competence.

Here are the sixteen essential entrepreneurial competence:

	Entrepreneurship Competence
Value Proposition	Value Proposition is the product or service you offer designed to solve problems for your customer.
Marketing/Market Focus	Marketing/Market Focus is researching your potential customers' demographics to find and understand their buying habits.
Start-Up	In the process of starting your business, you should self-fund your startup and then seek out alternative funding when you can create a growth strategy.
Entrepreneurship Self-Awareness	Entrepreneurship self-awareness is recognizing your strengths, weaknesses, and timing. It is essential to know when you need to engage or hire an accountant, lawyer, insurance agent, marketing specialist, web page designer, or another professional.
Surround yourself with advisors and mentors	Launching and growing a business is difficult, and more than half of those who try will fail within five years. No one person can have all the knowledge, experience, or even perspective to handle every business situation. Gain knowledge from others.
SCORE mentor	Find a SCORE mentor. A SCORE mentor is a mentor that provides small businesses with training, meetings, and resources that are designed for a start-up business and existing small business. The services are free — just visit www.SCORE.org.
Write a business plan	Starting a business is difficult and risky; it is easy to spend all your time and resources. Before you start, decide what type of business you will have and develop a small business plan.

Start-up cost	Start-up costs are the actual expenses that you need to start, grow, and maintain your business. It is good to understand how much money you need to open and to operate your business.
Sweat Equity	Being a small business owner is one of the most challenging jobs around. In a recent survey, 40 percent of small business owners said they do not take vacations and have their money tied up in their business. Make sure you are committed to the process of being an entrepreneur because it is not for everyone.
Passion	Being a business owner can be very lonely, and there are not enough hours in the day to accomplish everything. You better have a passion for what you are doing. Money cannot be the sole reason for starting your company.
Network	Join or develop a mastermind networking group and organizations that are in the same industry. The most important thing is to surround yourself with the right people.
Camaraderie	It is critical that you find and connect with other business owners, helping you develop your business.
There is No Set Path	There is no set path. A profitable business requires change. Your ideas will evolve along the way, and that is okay. Keep refining your product or services.
Everyone Has Unsolicited Advice	Everyone has an opinion regarding how you should run your business, although they have never been in your shoes. Even people with 9-5 jobs will often attempt to tell you what your business needs. Remember always to stay humble and focused.
Early Success is Temporary Luck	Early Success is luck. So, when you experience it, stay focused on the mission and vision of your company.
Family Comes First	Your family should always come first. You are going to take significant risks but never risk your family.

9. Personal Branding Competence

Personal Branding is defined as 'the system whereby you, your career, and expertise reflect personal type of workforce influence." Personal Branding is a revolutionary concept that keeps evolving. With fierce competition in the global marketplace, finding a job or even starting a company can feel like a nightmare. Today, jobs are constantly being outsourced or eliminated. For this reason, personal branding is vital to marketplace success. Personal branding is recognizing that you are your flag-ship product and if you want to be successful you must market yourself to others.

Developing a personal brand is future of the workforce development. Branding includes the entirety of Hustle Culture Skills, Competencies, and Principals. Theoretically, most of what you learn and implement from Hustle Culture will help you establish your brand. The secret is that branding is both what you do online and offline. The right image can transform an individual's life or can wreck a person's career hopes. Thus, spending an adequate quantity of time in developing your brand can be a precious commodity to your future.

Note: Whatever you post on social media is your brand. Be careful of what you post it could be used against you.

10. Self Maintenance Competence

Self-maintenance is the process by which you physically, mentally and emotionally maintain yourself. This includes diet, exercise, counseling and life coaching. You must learn how to love and take care of your body, emotions and your mind. The idea of self-maintenance also includes how you manage relationships and family. It is critical that you realize that you are the only you that you will ever have; you must take care of yourself! You can hinder the purpose and plan for your life if you fail to maintain yourself.

Pillar 3-Hustle Culture Principles

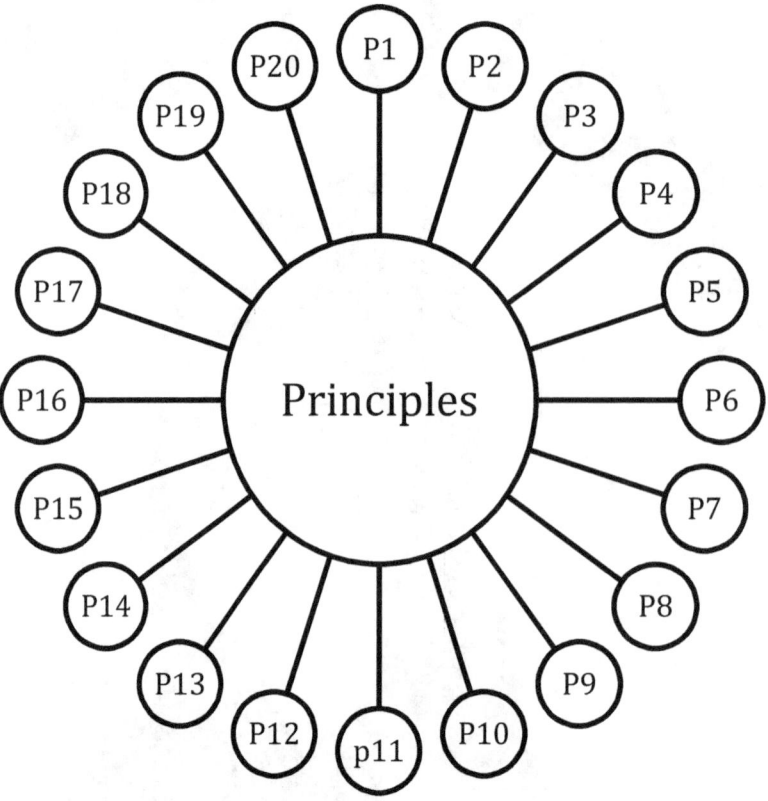

What are the truths that govern your life? We have covered the Hustle Culture Skills that are needed to master the workforce. We have also covered the Hustle Culture Competencies that will allow you to increase and enhance your skills. Now we must dig deeper to discuss the Hustle Culture Principles that frame Hustle Culture Hunger Mindset. Hustle Culture Principles are fundamental truths, codes, and thoughts that serve as your foundation for personal and professional success.

The Hustle Culture Principles are twenty statements of beliefs, behaviors, and ideas shared by millions of successful people. I discovered that every successful CEO, athlete, entertainer, innovator, religious leader, and creative all share a mixture of the Hustle Culture Principles.

Regardless of how well you attempt to implement Hustle Culture Skills and Competencies, they are all governed by your Hustle Culture Principles. It is often stated that we are the total of our thoughts. Therefore, nothing in your life spontaneously happens because your life is the refection of your thoughts. Everything you believe from health, faith, family, and finances manifests itself in your thought pattern.

These principles packaged together program your HumanOS. All principles are programmed codes that determine your daily thoughts and operations. This coding is so powerful that it causes unseen thoughts to express themselves in the visible world

through your actions. Your principles are either manifesting your dreams or nightmares.

You were born to be successful! You were created to achieve your goals and purpose! It is your faulty coded principles that keep you from excelling.

Successful people are not lucky! They manifest a daily, intentional effort to implement the right coding. In the next few pages, I will share twenty core principles shared by individuals that are living out their purpose, mission, and vision.

Principle One: Live and Release Your Pearls of Possibility

Let us be honest if you are reading this book, you want a wonderful life. Regardless of where you are in life, you have a passion to be great. You want to live a life that is beyond your current reality. You are hungry for more! Inside of you is a hunger and thirst for greatness. As you have been reading this manual, you have experienced the pulsating yearnings for lifelong fulfillment that would enable you to quit your job, start your business, or whatever your heart envisions. I call these pulses, this hunger, and thirst, your Pearls of Possibility.

Pearls of Possibility are the finest and the most precious seeds of potential power, capacity, endowment, and ability that you have. It is a spiritual egg that carries the genetic particles of your dreams, visions, purpose, innovations, and/or ideas.

Everything that you do in life should manifest your Pearls of Possibility. No matter if it is personal or business-related, your Pearls of Possibility are your seeds to greatness. The only way for you to experience greatness is for you to have a dream, a vision, and a purpose.

Those who live a life of greatness sow their Pearls of Possibility in the world. Therefore, cherish your Pearls of Possibility and continue to nourish them and encourage them to grow. Your current circumstances might not be favorable at this moment, but if you continue to live and sow your Pearls of Possibility, your life will change.

Please read my book Pearls of Possibility, because it explores the science of growing your Pearls of Possibility.

Principle Two: Hustlers Fellowship with Hustlers

The people you fellowship with and hang with will influence you and your thoughts. This is simple science. Social scientists have documented how much we affect each other's thinking and beliefs. There is empirical evidence that we, as humans, have a strong tendency to adopt the same goals, feelings, and ideas of those people that we spend time with.

If you hang out with pessimistic and lazy people, you are likely to feel as cynical, and perform as poorly, as they do overtime. Science even shows, on a macro level, if you hang out with obese people, you are 45% more likely to be obese. How much more is that when it relates to finance, business, and Hustle?

Your friends are a snapshot of your future. Your thinking, principles, and HumanOS are a parallel image of your friendships and your thoughts. Hustlers fellowship with Hustlers because it affects their principles. My Dad says, "Your Net worth is based on your Network!"

Principle Three: Continue to Always Have Tikvah

TIKVAH, which is Hebrew for hope, means to have an expectation. It comes from the root word kavah, meaning to bind together, collect, to expect: – tarry, wait (for, on, upon). To never let go of hope. Daily apply hope and faith to produce your vision for your life. Uses hope to create an inward mentality that is driven by extreme confidence to materialize your dreams, visions, purpose, innovations, and/or ideas.

If you are struggling in the area of hope, read my book *Tikvah*. This book identifies a step-by step plan on how to release and grow your faith and hope.

Principle Four: Have a Spirit of Excellence-Give it Your All

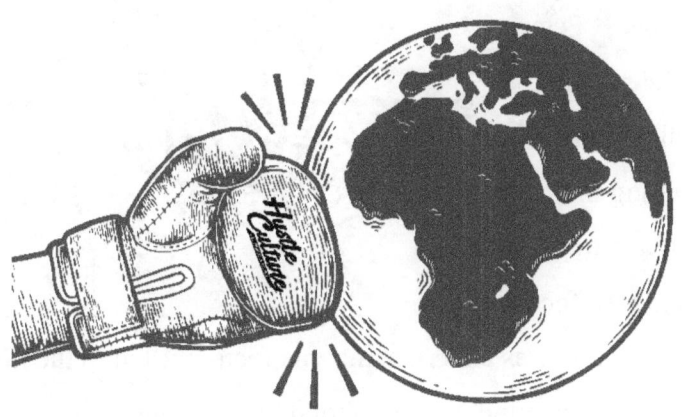

Nothing comes easy. The more effort you put into achieving a goal, the faster and better the outcome will be. Excellence creates intentional levels of favor and develops an excellent reputation to solidify your business and personal brand.

Principle Five: Have Faith to Drown

One of my favorite stories about the power of faith is the story of Peter walking on water. In this story, the Master Jesus accumulated a following of more than 5,000 people. These people followed Jesus everywhere. It was during this time that Jesus did some unbelievable things like healing and feeding them. One night after the Master had finished giving hope to the crowd, he told his students to get into their boats and go to the other side of a large lake. He assured them that he would eventually catch up with them later. After large group eventually departed, the Master went up into a mountain to pray and meditate. That evening, while the Master was praying and meditating, a massive storm rolled in. This was a storm so violent that the Master's students were alarmed and afraid. When the Master saw his students in despair, he went out to them by walking on water.

When the Master appeared to his students, he was scarcely visible in the twilight. The students assumed that a monster, or a ghost, was approaching, walking on water. Recognizing that they were afraid, the Master yelled out to them from a distance and informed them that he was approaching; therefore, they had no reason to fear.

Peter, one of the Master's students, was so inspired when he heard the Master's voice that he immediately converted his fear into extreme faith. He wanted to walk on water. Peter yelled out to the Master, "Master if it is you, tell me to meet you on the water." The Master responded, "Peter, come on out." Immediately, Peter sprang out of the boat and started walking on water towards the Master. During his miraculous walk on the water, a strong wind jolted him. Peter began to lose focus on the miracle and the blessing that he was experiencing; his focus shifted to the things around him. Instantly, fear attacked his mind, and he started to sink. Out of compassion and love, the Master pulled Peter up and instructed him regarding his lack of faith.

Prolific spiritual teachers have told this story millions of times. The standard synopsis has always been Peter's lack of faith and not keeping his eyes on the Master. Every summary has been that if Peter had only held his eyes on the Master, he would have never started sinking. As right as these prolific men and women are, they neglect to see the full picture of the victorious moment that Peter experienced over fear. The image that we forget is that Peter had the faith to drown. That he was 100% committed to the call, and he dared to believe. These are a few things that we learn from Peter's victorious moment in releasing faith and starving fear.

Only 8% of people are willing to follow that inward call to walk out on their faith. True faith is a real belief, despite the noticeably clear reality of present uncertainty and tremendous odds. Nevertheless, many people fear venturing out into a world of faith when the odds are uncertain. Understand that Peter was not the only one in that boat. There were eleven other men, all of whom never attempted to get out of the ship. Eleven men never tried to walk on water; instead, they were willing to accept their reality of impending death. They were fearful and faithless spectators. 92% of people are so afraid that they watch just to see other people's faith in action. They are the commentators and analysts that always have something to say. They are the dream killers.

So, why would Peter get out of the boat? Peter was willing to drown just for an opportunity to change his reality. Without certainty or planning, he followed the call. He

was ready to die for something that he believed. He believed in the Master, and he believed in the impossible and ignored the odds.

Hustle Culture Hunger Mindset is about having a passion for something for which you are willing to drown. Whatever your passion is, the only way you will be able to actualize it is to be ready to drown for it. That means facing your fear and accepting the reality of failure while embracing the hope of achieving the impossible.

You must be 100% Committed

Peter's first steps were a testament to his 100% commitment to his faith. As soon as he stepped out of the boat, he was all in. He did not have a Plan B. He did not have a life jacket. All he had was 100% faith and 100% commitment. Many of us are looking for turnkey opportunities in faith or an easy way to enter Hustle Culture. We want the glory without the risk of failure, rejection, misunderstanding, and poverty. Faith is not faith if it does not have an element of risk. Peter's commitment to get out and follow the call serves as an example of releasing one's Pearls of Possibility and having a Hustle Culture Hunger Mindset. Peter's faith was released when he exercised the courage to face his fear and his willingness to challenge his current reality in hopes of a better tomorrow. Destroying fear and empowering your faith is a Hustle Culture Way. Hustle Culture Hunger Mindset is the 100% commitment to your faith and your Pearls of Possibility.

Dare to Believe

History does not tell us the conversation that might have occurred between Peter and the others on the boat. We do know that he alone made a step of faith. Peter's story only serves as a reminder that releasing your Pearls of Possibility and living a Hustle Culture Lifestyle can lead you to a lonely place. Everyone around you may not understand, nor will they actively support you releasing your Pearls of Possibility. They will, however, be watching to see if you drown. You must dare to believe in what you are doing, even when you are alone. You need faith; it is what will keep you pressing and going forward when the world around you is full of despair and lacks hope. Unbelief and doubt kill the dreamer inside of us and disrupts the Hustle

Culture Hunger Mindset. That is why people who walk in faith are unique; they are Hustle Culture People. They are alive inside because they dare to believe.

Peter illustrates that the power to walk on water is in us and around us if we have a Hustle Culture Hunger Mindset.

Principle Six: Chill Out, Be Amazing, Be In-Control

Chill Out, Be Amazing, and Be in Control! Hustle Culture Hunger Mindset is rooted in self-awareness, being comfortable being you, and being in control of yourself. When you reach a self-awareness level, you will have a deeper intuitive understanding of who you are. Think about it; with self-awareness, you can identify your personality, personal strengths, and weaknesses. You can clearly articulate your thoughts, ideas, and beliefs. You are emotionally secure. With self-awareness, you are able to look at the world differently and be in control of your destiny. There are three things you can do to unleash your self-awareness:

- Control Your Mind, Emotions, and Thoughts.
- Focus Your Attention, Emotions, and Energy on your goals.
- Be Aware of your Thoughts, Behavior, and Words.

Without Self Awareness, it is virtually impossible to chill out, be unique, and be in control. You cannot live your life for other people. Take a moment to identify what is unique and special about yourself. Do you spend time daily celebrating the beauty of being unique? You will find that with self-awareness, you can accept yourself. When you can reach a place of Self-Awareness, you will be empowered to be amazing. Take the time to regularly reaffirm that you are, in fact, skilled, knowledgeable, and wonderfully made.

Principle Seven: It Is Never Too Late

Many of us spend way too much time trying to measure our lives based on other people's perceptions. Think about it: from the time we wake up until the time we get to bed, we are continually being bombarded with others' perceptions of who we are supposed to be. These perceptions are not facts but are illusions and false standards. It does not matter how old you are; there is a plan for your life; however, you must work towards that plan. Society often sets a timeline with which we gauge our success. This unspoken timeline creates an unwarranted urgency to achieve some level of materialistic or social success at a certain age. Hustle Culture is not the result of real-time activities. Hustle Culture is the combustible collision of purpose, destiny, time, individual skills, competencies, and principles. Greatness, success achievement of goals happens at different times for different people. Below are the names of people who became successful after the age of forty:

- Vera Wang
- Donald Fisher
- Stan Lee
- Gary Heavin
- Robin Chase
- Samuel L. Jackson
- Sam Walton
- Henry Ford
- Jack Weil
- Rodney Dangerfield
- Momofuku Ando
- Julia Child
- Jack Cover
- Betty White
- Taikichiro Mori
- Tim and Nina Zagat
- Ray Kroc
- Harland Sanders

Use this list as a source of encouragement and reminder that your life is never finished, and those who aspire to chase after their dreams will reap the benefits in time. Ancient sages used to teach that greatness takes time and undergoes levels of disappointments and setbacks; that life's journey is designed to develop the character that leads to success. For some, success might require forty years for others twenty. It is your life and your journey; be consistent with your purpose and you will manifest your destiny! Your gifts will make room for you when the time is right. Stop thinking and adjusting your life based on current reality. Your current reality is merely temporary, if you keep Hustling forward.

Principle Eight: Take Risk

If your last year looks like this year, then you are not Hustling. The pursuit of the Hustle will always keep you in a perpetual state of transition. If it is a new business or project, greatness requires that you take risks. Why? People who desire to be the best shun the very appearance of being average. Ordinary people work to find a situation where they are comfortable but those that inspire to be the best dare to seek new adventures that add to their caliber of life. They celebrate the milestone, but they re-calibrate and go after the next adventure.

Hustle Culture requires you to take risks; this is exactly what ordinary people are afraid to do. You might ask why risk-taking is so important? The answer is quite simple: when you accept risks, you are in a state of evolving and becoming mentally stronger. Risk fuels the Hustle Culture Hunger Mindset. When you take risk, you learn and grow as a person. With every risk, there is an opportunity for growth. The result of risk-taking is that you learn a new skill, develop new competencies, and strengthen your core principles. Risk-taking strengthens your faith by forcing you to confront your fears. When you face your fears, you enhance both your drive and ambition. It also makes you more resilient because you must persevere above self-imposed limitations. Taking risks also illuminates your purpose and opens your mind to levels of innovation and creativity.

Principle Nine:
Everyday Must Count

The average person will live to be eighty years old. So, how many days do you have to fulfill your purpose? If you take your current age and subtract it from 80 and multiply that number by 365, you end up with the average amount of days that you have left in your life. Time is a spiritual mandate; therefore, "Everyday Must Count." You do not have time to shuck and jive with your purpose. **Your life is like fog: it is heavy and dense; however, it dissipates over time.**

Your life is short and can be viewed as a narrow window of potential purpose. Therefore, you must fight to remain focused on purpose and refuse to waste the gift of time. A stated earlier in the manual, Hustle Culture is rooted in leveraging time. It is about avoiding the pitfalls that tend to consume our time. Life and death are actual realities, and therefore wasting time is not an option. Your life and your legacy will be remembered by how you fulfilled your purpose during your lifetime.

Principle Ten: It is the LIL (Loyalty is Life) Thing

Loyalty is Life! Loyalty is more than just a phase or a statement; it is a way of living. Loyalty is an unyielding commitment and dedication to another that is rooted in respect and trust.

In this current age, loyalty is not discussed, especially among those who work white-collar jobs. Loyalty is often seen as something that only gangsters and gangs do. However, loyalty is a vital principle to live by. Loyalty must be earned and nurtured over time. It should never be taken advantage of or taken for granted. In many ways, loyalty represents a form of human capital; it gives you leverage because you can predict the actions of those people in whom you have trust and confidence. Over the years, I have found that loyalty defines a person and reveals a person's integrity and character. Here are some rules about loyalty:

1. **Be loyal to your past! Never discuss people or bad mouth people from your past. Forgive them and move on.**
2. **If you cannot be loyal to your romantic partner, family, or friends, you cannot be a person that is loyal to business affairs.**
3. **Loyalty is an inward code that you live by.**
4. **Never trust or develop loyalty towards individuals who gossip.**
5. **Always be loyal to yourself and never give up on your dreams and Pearls of Possibility.**
6. **Never spend time with ungrateful people. Ungrateful people tend to be disloyal.**

7. Foster relationships with other loyal people.
8. Create an environment where your partner has nothing bad to say about you.
9. Everyone does not deserve the right to be in your inner circle.
10. Be respected based on your loyalty and actions towards others.
11. Blessing comes to people who are loyal.
12. Loyalty creates a legacy that everyone remembers.
13. When you are loyal is makes is easier to make decision and to do the right thing.
14. Deeper relationships with the people we love are a result of loyalty.

Principle Eleven: A Changed Mind is a Changed Life

Very few people are lucky enough to have overnight success. Therefore, for the majority of people, succuss is the result of making the mental decision to take steps towards your purpose, vision, and mission. **So, in order to have a Hustle Culture Hunger Mindset, you MUST change your MIND!**

Your first step begins with a mind that is "made up." There is tremendous power when a person has an unyielding mindset. When your mind is made up, it will help to alleviate distractions and frustrations.

Principle Twelve: Develop Productive Habits

I have found that developing productive habits is the key to the continuous and persistent achievement of goals. For this reason, it is essential when pursuing your goals to have the tools in place to maintain the stamina needed to thrive in Hustle Culture. Motivation doesn't work. Change only comes from knowing what you want to do and having a passion for doing what is necessary to create that change; including, developing the types of habits needed to make those changes. Having productive habits are the rails that keep your dreams on track. Here are some tips to help you supercharge your productive habits:

1. *Create a vision board and fill it with images of your desired end. Fill that vision board with images of things that you want. It can be tangible items like cars, a house, or clothing. It can also be intangible items like peace, passion, harmony, health, and prosperity. If you can picture it and visualize it, then it is possible.*

2. *GET ANGRY! I do not mean to get upset; I mean, fighting mad. This kind of blackout rage will cause you to get into the ring of life and contend for something greater than your current reality. The truth is, if you desire to change your life for the better, then you must get angry about where you are at in the present. Having a blasé attitude towards change will not create enough fuel to energize you to change your reality. Passion, which means to suffer, is what is needed to develop a strong desire within you. No one will tell you that real change demands an actual fight or that all dream makers, at some point, had to get angry about their current reality and be willing to fight for more. Successful people commit themselves to do whatever it takes to change their current reality.*

3. *Respect Time! Time is the solitary thing that you and I can never get back. It is the Universe's NONRENEWABLE resource. Therefore, you should never squander it. We all have things in our lives that distract us. I call these things time wasters. If you desire to make your dreams a reality, you must make the most of your most precious resource – time. To this end, you must put an end to all the mindless drifting, destroy things that are irrelevant in your life, and find a balance between work and pleasure. For example, television, social media, video games, and hanging out are non-essential activities that will not help dreams come into fruition; therefore, time committed to these activities should be planned and used sparingly. Remember, no one knows how much time is allotted to them while living on this earth; thus, one should make sure that each day counts for something.*

4. *Go against the norm. Hustle Culture requires you to create your own fortune. 90% of people are mindless zombies who follow the herd instead of making their way. They are time consumers and dream eaters. If you want to change your reality and achieve a greater success level, you cannot follow the herd and go where everyone else goes or do what everyone else does.*

5. *Destroy your fear. Faith and fear cannot occupy the same space. Fear is a very nasty, destructive parasite that eats dreams and kills motivation. So, release faith!*

Principle Thirteen: Collaboration

As people are becoming increasingly branded in their desired craft, collaboration is a principle that is becoming essential. Collaboration is when a group of people come together and contribute their expertise to achieve a shared goal, task, or objective.

Collaboration is the foundation for teamwork. How well you collaborate with others will impact your life. Whatever you inspire to do is going to require some level of synergy and collaboration. Your dreams are not designed to be accomplished alone; therefore, it is critical to collaborate with people to release your Pearls of Possibility.

People who work well with others are likely to be more economically prosperous, more culturally aligned, and have high level of personal growth. I am a firm believer that if you let go of ego, collaboration will change in your life. You have the expertise, but you must stay in your lane! Collaboration is using others to maximize what you are good at, so you can focus on the mission and vision instead of trying to complete tasks alone.

Principle Fourteen: Can't Stop, Won't Stop Mentality

If you are a Hustle Culture Citizen (entrepreneur, leader, etc.), you will realize that your success cannot rely upon others' suppositions, opinions, and fears. Like a breeze, people's opinions change. To win at any undertaking, you should stay the course - no matter what the expense! You must have a **Can't Stop, Won't Stop Mentality.** Here are some tips to help you:

1. **Maintain a strategic distance from negativity.** Adverse, non-hustle minded people will hinder your success. These negative people can be family and friends. Words and energy from outsiders with whom you have relationships can breed bad Hustle Culture environment. I am not saying to avoid relationships with these people, like family and friends, but I am suggesting limiting the types of discussion you have with them.

2. **Build Yourself Up.** You must be your biggest fan and cheerleader! No, I do not mean for you to puff yourself up proudly; instead, you can be your best wellspring of support and empowerment. Invest in yourself through meditation and prayer. Study the lifestyles of different business icons who have gone before you. Use books, empowerment tools and historical figures as role models. **Think Positive, Speak Positive and Be Positive!**

3. **Return to Your Foundation.** Should you wind up faltering, remember the things that encouraged you to release your Pearls of Possibility. Your foundation is your Hustle Culture Skills, Competencies and Principles.

Principle Fifteen: Find Your Fight

It has been said that Earnest Henley's whole career as a writer can be viewed through the lens of, what I believe is, the most potent poem ever written, *Invictus* (see resources).

Historians account that the writer, Earnest Henley, was inspired by his leg amputation. During the recovery, he began to reflect on his early childhood and the unbelievable poverty that he experienced. The result of this reflection was the creation of the poem that paints a picture of triumph when undergoing extreme adversity.

Invictus means to be "unconquerable" or "undefeated. When will you decide to be Invictus? When will you fight back? You will experience extreme adversity - times where you will feel beaten by circumstances, and you will be mentally and physically exhausted. You will feel as though you are facing a storm that is impossible to endure. It is in these moments that you must find your Invictus Hustle. Your Invictus Hustle compels you to continue the advance towards your dreams and visions. There are times when losing is not an option; instead, you must be Invictus.

I cannot imagine the pain that Earnest Henley experienced when his leg was being removed. However, his words are an affirmation to get up regardless of the obstacles. The Hustle doesn't come without a fight, so you have to dig deep and discover the power to command your destiny. As it did for Earnest Henley, the fight through adversity will give you the power to captain your future.

Your fate is up to you! You have the power to either be a victim or a victor. Your ability to win in life is fixed on the words that you say, your daily habits, and actions. You have a responsibility to activate your Pearls of Possibility even in times of trouble. You are a winner, but you must fight for it! You might be bloody and bruised, but you are still winning! There are four things you can do to release an Invictus Hustle.

1. *Reconnect to the Mission and Vision – Why are you doing what you are doing?*
2. *Develop a Plan and execute it -- What are you going to do?*
3. *Prioritize Time and Energy to achieve your mission.*
4. *Stay Focused.*

Principle Sixteen: Healthy Lifestyle

A healthy body is the key to enjoying life and achieving personal fulfillment. This principle activates all the twenty Hustle Culture Principles. By eating healthy food and challenging your brain with exercise, you can activate all the other Hustle Culture Principles.

Principle Seventeen: Habits-The Making or Breaking Factor

Everybody wants peace in their mind, good health, and financial security. Therefore, you need to develop the positive habits to achieve them. It takes extreme discipline and time to develop good habits. Whatever your goal is, you must have the corresponding habits to make it a reality.

Principle Eighteen: Do You and Be Epic About It

I was never much a fan of Shakespeare in high school, but I became more of a fan as I experienced life's peaks and valleys. Life has taught me the importance of Hustling to become the best you, while doing you. Polonius, in Shakespeare's *Hamlet*, said, "To thine own self is true." It is not enough to just say these words; instead, they must become your day-to-day mantra. True success is a balance between Hustle and not selling out. Most people never reach a point in life where they conduct their lives based on their self-interest and destiny. They work hard to earn material wealth but along the way they sell themselves short. The only way you can thrive in Hustle Culture is to be committed to war for yourself and be epic about living your life, not anyone else's.

What is your vision for your life? What trauma, rejection, or situation has attempted to disrupt that vision? The world is full of dream catchers and vision killers. Dream catchers and vision killers will either push you to be great, or they will steal greatness from you.

Dream catchers and vision killers can be situations, experiences, and/or people in our lives. Dream catchers and vision killers will make you feel like your Hustle is impossible.

They may cause you to feel rejected, inadequate and inferior. Dream catchers and vision killers are not necessarily bad in and of themselves, but they are infected with negativity, pessimism and unbelief. The only remedy to their venomous poison is unapologetic commitment to be true to yourself and to be who you were created to be.

So, the question is, who were you created to be? All of the information in this book point to a very powerful but important question of personal identity. Personal identity is the vaccine to keep you immune from a life filled with negativity, pessimism and unbelief. Do you have what it takes to discover the cure for a deadly disease? Are you the musical artist that will make a song that will be a soundtrack for a movement or a theme song for a generation? Are you the next President of the United States? Are you the educator that will reform education? The only person that can answer the question of destiny is you.

Being true to yourself is the elixir to fighting low self-esteem. When you have low self-esteem, you buy into the propaganda and psychology of the dream catchers and vision killers. When you are not confident in who you are, you amplify your weakness and dismiss your strengths.

If you want to win and excel in Hustle Culture, shift your focus to the things that you are good at and that are good about you.

Doing you and being epic about it has nothing to do with your appearance, socioeconomic status, or career. Doing You is a by-product of unapologetically living who you were created to be while releasing the genius within.

Principle Nineteen: Learn to Soar

There comes a time when you must let everything go in order to become your best. If you ask anyone who is living their dreams, they will tell you that it cost them something. It might not have been the same thing for each person, but the reality remains the same – they had to give up something or somebody. They had to give up the burdens that kept them from soaring to higher heights. Your life is like an airplane with a luggage limit capacity. Anytime you go over the luggage limit, it becomes unsafe to fly. If you want to fly safely, you must get rid of the luggage that keeps you grounded. It is imperative to eliminate any excess weight that will restrain you from soaring. There are ten pieces of luggage you must drop before you can soar:

- Measuring your life by the past
- Envying people
- Surrounding yourself with people who refuse to soar
- Second-guessing yourself, your purpose, and why you were created
- The fear of the Hustle
- Allowing your hunger and passion for purpose to die
- Having conversations without action
- Equating success to money
- Living an inauthentic self
- Living a life that does not make you happy
- Participating in negative talking and thinking
- Thinking that you are not important
- Not loving yourself
- Allowing others to mentally, physically, and verbally abuse you
- Not taking care of your body

Principle Twenty: Have a Clearly Defined Mission and Vision

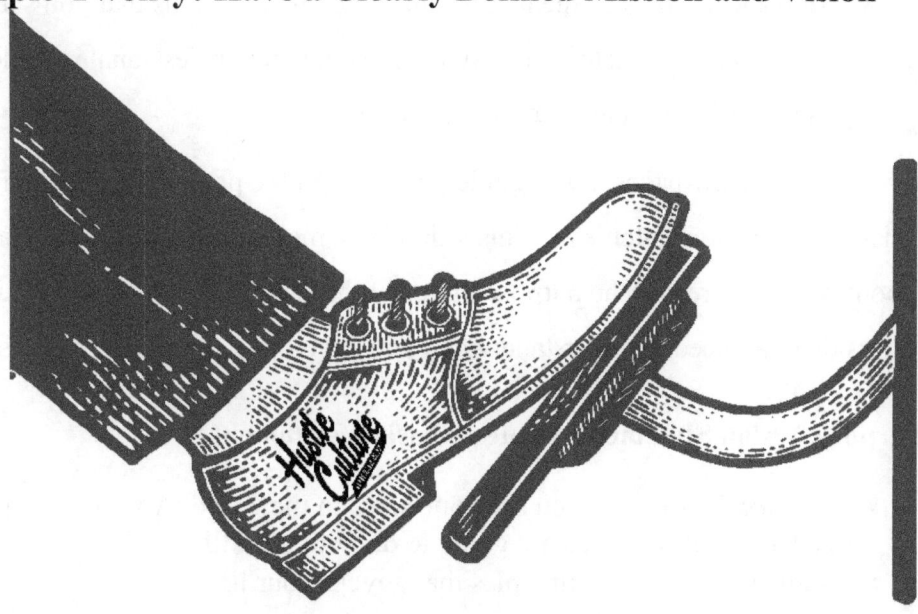

Having a clear mission and vision is the most significant principle in the Hustle Culture arsenal. While the idea of having a mission and vision may be outlandish to you; corporations often use vision and mission statements to help them plan their goals and develop strategic business strategies. When developing a Hustle Culture Lifestyle, having a written personal vision and mission statement serves as a critical strategy in personal and workforce development. Clearly defined mission and vision statements will allow you to develop personal goals that will help you to implement the skills, competencies, and principles that have been covered in this book. It will also guide you in developing action steps that will help you transform your life.

The implementation of this Hustle Culture Principles is a secret weapon that most people do not have. The advantage of these principles is the creation process. Creating and having a personal mission and vision statement requires that you undergo a thorough evaluation of who you are, your core values and what you were created to do. The end result of this deep dive is the development of a series of affirmational statements that will guide your implementation of Hustle Culture Skills, Competencies and Principles.

The next series of pages will help you create and develop your personal mission and vision statements. Through a series of exercises, you will clarify your deepest values and aspirations. The goal is to help you to develop both your mission and vision, while helping you integrate them into your day-to-day planning.

Mission and vision statements are your fundamental truths that you should use to govern your life. They help you to avoid personal and professional roadblocks, and it give you the ability articulate to others your Hustle.

In the next few pages, I will guide you through the process of developing your mission and vision statements. This will take some time and will force you to think about who you are and the purpose of your life. So, let us get started! There are a few terms that you need to understand when you develop your mission and vision:

Purpose, Vision Statement, Values, Mission Statement.

- **Vision:** This is how you see your place in the world. A vision is written statement of what you are going to do with your life.
- **Values:** The moral principles that govern your life.

- **Purpose:** The reason why you are living.
- **Mission:** The defining action and task that you are going to implement as the results of your vision and purpose. It is a description of what your life should focus on. It combines your vision, purpose, and values with how you use your time, resources, and life.

Example
Vision: I see a world that is filled with a generation of people empowered and fulfilling their purpose and destiny.
My purpose: To impact and empower the world that I live in by empowering people's lives.
Mission: I will set new trends as I vow to maintain to be on the cutting edge as a generational innovator. With all my strength, will, and with my last breath, I shall educate humanity and entertain the world. I commit myself to extend hope to all generations and to extend love to societies forgotten. I will create a family dynasty for which my seed and future generation may build upon the essence of my integrity, humility, prosperity, and love for humanity and God. I will be a restorer of the breach. I will succeed when others fail and win regardless of the cost as I align my life to fulfill destiny and purpose. *I shall die knowing that I have fulfilled God's Plan. I never let anything undone, and that I ran my life's race and finished its course. -K.A. Perkins*

How to Find Your Purpose?

The first step to developing a mission and vision statement begins with finding your purpose. Discovering your purpose is not easy. Several barriers can prevent you from realizing your purpose. Some of these barriers are:

- *Cultural and environmental pressure*
- *Money and position*
- *The illusion of age (You missed the opportunity because of your age.)*
- *Lack of exposure to opportunities*
- *Lack of skills, competences, and principles.*

Before you start to develop your purpose, you must believe that you have a purpose. You must have faith that you were created to live a life of happiness, joy, and fulfillment. If you believe that, then there are eight things that you can do to find your purpose.

1. *Mentally envision your life without barriers and ask yourself, what would it look like?*
2. *Write down any job that you would do for free.*
3. *Write down all the things that make you happy.*

4. *Cultivate your hobbies.*
5. *Start doing what you are good at and passionate about.*
6. *Spend time reading and learning.*
7. *Listen and take clues from what others have to say about you as it relates to gifts and talents.*
8. *Find fulfillment in yourself.*

Finding your purpose is not an overnight process. Discovering your purpose takes time. The key to developing your purpose is to define your version of success. Do what you love. Focus on your passion, and your meaning will manifest itself. Take the time to identify your passions, values, and goals. Make sure that you take the action steps that will propel you closer to your purpose every day.

Purpose Statement

_____
_____
_____
_____
_____

Now that you have discovered your purpose. Write your purpose as a statement of affirmation. Write your purpose down, post it in your office or in your bathroom. The next step is to develop your vision statement.

How to Define Your Vision

Your vision statement is how you see yourself in the world. When you close your eyes, what do you dream? What is the future you see? Your vision is your aspiration of hope.

A vision statement is a short snapshot of who you are. It is a statement of your desired future. Your vision statement is the beacon of light that you follow. It is your fundamental guidepost that you often visit to keep your life focus and on track.

Your vision sticks with you; it does not change. A good vision statement envelops your purpose so that it expresses your ideas, beliefs, and the optimal conditions for your life.

Personal Vision Statements Should Be:

- Easily remembered
- Inspiring and uplifting
- Easy to articulate to others.

Here are some examples of vision statements that meet the above criteria:

To be a teacher. And to be known for inspiring my students to be more than they thought they could be. -Oprah Winfrey

"To have fun in [my] journey through life and learn from [my] mistakes."-Richard Branson

If you look at these vision statements and investigate the lives of the individuals to whom they belong, you will discover that their vision statements reflect their individual purposes. What is most remarkable about each of their vision statements that neither are connected to money. A vision statement is more significant than monetary gain. Your vision connects to legacy and purpose. Vision statement transcends money and all material things; they are the unapologetic defining statement that drives you to personal greatness.

How to Develop a Personal Vision Statement

Developing a vision statement is something that every person needs to do, regardless of career choice or profession. You must discover and understand what you stand for, what achievements you want to make, and what you want to be known for.

The first step to developing a personal vision statement is to answer some pertinent questions thoughtfully and honestly.

- What do you value?
- What are your aspirations?
- What talents do you possess?
- What accomplishments do you want to leave behind at the end of your life?

Think deeply about these questions and respond honestly because these answers are the foundation upon which you will build your vision statement. All the answers might not come immediately, especially if you are having these thoughts for the first time. Write down the answers that come to you and continue to ponder until you answer all the questions.

What do you value?

_____
_____
_____
_____
_____
_____

What are your aspirations?

_____
_____
_____
_____
_____
_____

What talents do you possess?

_____
_____
_____
_____
_____
_____

What accomplishments do you want to leave behind at the end of your life?

_____
_____
_____
_____
_____
_____

If you want to have a powerful vision statement, you must be honest with yourself. You must honestly answer each of the above questions, even if you do not like the answers you discover. Hustle Culture is about to change, so set aside your ego and embrace your vulnerability because it lays your truth.

As you put your responses together, you will find a pattern or consistent theme in these responses. These words or answers hold the key to unlock the things you are sincerely passionate about.

Anyone who has defined their vision can express it in a brief statement that carries the benefits and the power of who they are and what they want to do. As we covered earlier, Oprah Winfrey's vision statement is simple but profound. Your vision statement expresses how you will spend the entirety of your life and what you will spend it doing.

Consider what actions you need to take to achieve a fulfilled life. Take a few moments and summarize how you want to serve yourself and humanity.

How do you want to serve yourself and humanity?

_____
_____
_____
_____
_____
_____
_____
_____
_____
_____
_____
_____
_____
_____
_____
_____
_____
_____

Understand that there is no template for a personal vision statement; there is no wrong or right vision statement. Whatever your vision might be, it is yours to articulate and live out.

Now Write Your Vision Statement Below!

Vision Statement
_____
_____
_____
_____

Identifying Your Values

Now that you have developed your vision statement, the next step is to identify your values. Your values are the controls that help you to steer your life in the direction of your vision. They are individual levers and switches that move and operate your vision for your life.

People have different value sets that they hold dear; you do too. The key is to identify them to develop your mission statement. Values are embedded codes of beliefs the moral characteristics that make up who you are. The more you allow your values to govern your life, the more likely you will be successful and happy.

Values are so crucial to success that when they are violated, it creates gateways to personal burnout and depression. It is through the lens of identified values that will help you through the Hustle Culture Process. Your values will keep aligned with your authentic self.

Your next assignment is to write down the values you hold dear. They could be values you already embody or look forward to having. Here is a value list to help you.

- Authenticity, Accountability, Adventure, Action
- Boldness, Balance
- Consistency, Community, Compassion, Calmness, Creativity, Courage
- Diversity, Dependability
- Endurance, Enthusiasm
- Faith, Freedom, Fairness, Frugality
- Generosity
- Honesty, Humility, Humor
- Integrity, Individuality, Innovation, Intuition, Intelligence
- Kindness
- Longsuffering, Longevity
- Maturity, Modesty, Moderation
- Open-mindedness, Originality, Optimism
- Professionalism, Peace, Principled
- Respect, Resilience
- Sincerity, Simplicity
- Tradition, Trustworthy
- Wisdom, Wealth

Carefully examine this list and select five or six values that are important to you. The values you pick make up what we call a value system.

Write your value system below:

Value System
_____
_____
_____

Mission Statements

Mission statements are the plans, actions, and priorities that drive your vision. The purpose of a mission statement is to summarize what you want to accomplish and why.

At this point, you have discovered and outlined your purpose, written your vision statement, and identified your value system; now, you can take all these elements and break them into writing your mission statements.

Mission Statement vs Vision Statement

Most people get the vision and mission statement confused. In comparison, a vision statement is a long-term aspiration that does not change. Unlike a mission statement, a vision statement provides foresight into purpose and plans. A mission statement is a short-term statement that summarizes elements of your vision statement into intentional and direct actions.

Tips
- A good mission statement provides a strategic plan that encompasses your personal vision statement.
- A good mission statement should only be revised every few years.
- Mission statements are short-term calculated measures.
- A mission statement should be revised when it is no longer appropriate or relevant.
- A good mission statement encompasses you value mix.

Mission statements are created though three unique phases:

Phase 1: Envision the Future
Phase 2: Craft A Mission Statement
Phase 3: Make Your Mission Important

In the next few pages, I will guide you through these five phases. Developing a mission statement is an extraordinarily complex and thought-provoking process. This process will require you to act and make reflections.

ACTION-means you need to do something.
REFLECTION- is the act of monitoring your thoughts and ideas.

There are several things that I want you to do as you develop your mission statement.
1. Take time to reflect as you go through the activities.
2. Take time connecting to your PEARLS OF POSSIBILITY.
3. This section was designed to stimulate your PEARLS OF POSSIBILITY; therefore, there will be times when you will experience certain feelings, thoughts, emotions, or moments of inspiration.
4. Once you have your mission statement make it apart of your daily life.

Mission Statement Phase 1: Envision the Future

YOUR CONVICTIONS ARE YOUR PASSIONS

What excites you about this world we live in? Is there something that angers you about it? Can you name three things that you are passionate about? What are the factors that motivate you?

Write three things that you are passionate about?
1._____
2._____
3._____

What three things would your closest friends say that you are passionate about?
1._____
2._____
3._____

How can you use what you are passionate about to impact the world around you? List at least three ways.
1._____
2._____
3._____

What are three factors that motivate you to use what you are passionate about to improve the lives of others?
1._____
2._____
3._____

Mission Statement Phase 2: Crafting A Mission Statement

Action Words That Shaping Your Future						
All missions require action. Action words can be categorized as verbs. The following list contains a series of verbs. Isolate three from every column based on how much they excite you. From there, list the top three.						
Accomplish	Compliment	Elect	Give	Measure	Pursue	Serve
Acquire	Compose	Embrace	Grant	Mediate	Realize	Share
Adopt	Conceive	Encourage	Heal	Model	Receive	Speak
Advance	Confirm	Endow	Hold	Mold	Reclaim	Stand
Affect	Connect	Engage	Host	Motivate	Reduce	Summon
Affirm	Consider	Engineer	Identify	Move	Refine	Support
Alleviate	Construct	Enhance	Illuminate	Negotiate	Reflect	Surrender
Amplify	Contact	Enlighten	Implement	Nurture	Reform	Sustain
Appreciate	Continue	Enlist	Improve	Open	Regard	Take
Ascend	Counsel	Enliven	Improvise	Organize	Relate	Tap
Associate	Create	Entertain	Inspire	Participate	Relax	Team
Believe	Decide	Enthuse	Integrate	Pass	Release	Touch
Bestow	Defend	Evaluate	Involve	Perform	Rely	Trade
Brighten	Delight	Excite	Keep	Persuade	Remember	Translate
Build	Deliver	Explore	Know	Play	Renew	Travel
Call	Demonstrate	Express	Labor	Possess	Resonate	Understand
Cause	Devise	Extend	Launch	Practice	Respect	Use
Choose	Direct	Facilitate	Lead	Praise	Restore	Utilize
Claim	Discover	Finance	Light	Prepare	Return	Validate
Collect	Discuss	Forgive	Live	Present	Revise	Value
Combine	Distribute	Foster	Love	Produce	Sacrifice	Venture
Command	Draft	Franchise	Make	Progress	Safeguard	Verbalize
Communicate	Dream	Further	Manifest	Promise	Satisfy	Volunteer
Compel	Drive	Gather	Master	Promote	Save	Work
Compete	Educate	Generate	Nature	Provide	Sell	Worship

First Puzzle Piece #1

Write down purposeful, exciting, and meaningful verbs.

1._____
2._____
3._____

Second Puzzle Piece #2

Now that you have your action verbs, review your purpose, vision statement, and values. Based on those four elements write a phrase or a statement that connects them using the action verbs. Write the phrases below:

_____
_____
_____
_____
_____
_____
_____

What you believe you were put on this earth to do needs to be the foundation of your mission statement?

Take the phrase and statement above and focus on what Social Economic Milieu that you want to be in. Your Social Economic Milieu is the atmosphere where you release your Hustle. Your Social Economic Milieu can be an environment where you can learn, opportunities to inspire others, places of service, or industries that you have an opportunity to impact. I have provided a list below for you to use or you can add your own.

Social Economic Milieu

This is a sample list of words that form your Social Economic Milieu. Take a moment to pick a few of them out or add some of your own that appeal to you. You will use them to create your mission statement.

1. Environment	2. Family Issues	3. Education
4. Media	5. Health Care	6. Elderly
7. Children	8. The Poor	9. The Homeless
10. Immigration	11. Energy	12. Agriculture
13. The Justice System	14. Parks & Recreation	15. Veterans
16. Substance Abuse	17. Nutrition	18. Law
19. Politics	20. Government	21. Youth
22. Roads & Bridges	23. Business	24. Non-profit Agency
25. Churches	26. Synagogues	27. Spirituality
28. The Ill & Disabled	29. Public Safety	30. Human Development
31. Infants	32. Child Protection	33. Child Care
34. Justice	35. Home Health Care	36. Water Rights
37. Tourism	38. Defense	39. Space Exploration
40. Computer Technology	41. Animal Rights	42. Animal Care
43. Animal Protection	44. Literacy	45. Border Issues
46. Civil Rights Issues	47. Sexuality Issues	48. Fashion
49. Art	50. Books	51. Music
52. Movies	53. Design	54. Sports
55. Food	56. Travel	57. Women's Issues
58. Gardening	59. Printing & Publishing	60. Performing Arts
61. Administration	62. Management	63. Labor Relations
64. Construction	65. Finance	66. Real Estate
67. Religion	68. Community	69. Development
70. Reproductive Issues	71. Research	72. Biotechnology
73. Broadcasting	74. News	75. Journalism

Third Puzzle Piece #3

Now narrow select the Social Economic Milieu that you are interested and write the names below in the space provided:

Social Economic Milieu 1:
_____
_____

Social Economic Milieu 2:
_____
_____

Putting the Puzzle Together

The mission statement you are putting together will be defined by this formula (the sum of the first, second, and third puzzle pieces will reveal your mission in life). Write you mission statement in the space below.

_____
_____
_____
_____
_____
_____
_____
_____
_____
_____
_____
_____
_____
_____
_____
_____
_____
_____

Phase 3: Make Your Mission Important

Now that you have crafted your Mission Statement it is critical that you emphasize its importance, and you daily communicate it to others. There are three things that you can do make sure you are making make your Mission Statement important.

Communicating Your Mission Statement

- Post It
- Speak It
- Become It

Putting it all together

Congratulations! You have achieved an incredible feat! By identifying your purpose, developing your vision statement, value system, and personal mission statement, you have a roadmap to success.

It is not enough to have these details; you must put them to work. Begin by keeping all of the elements visible. Publish or print your values, mission, and vision statement somewhere you can always see them and be inspired by them to act.

When your vision and mission is visible, it will help to be accountable. The difference between the most successful people and those who spend months or years without tangible achievements that they make their mission statement important.

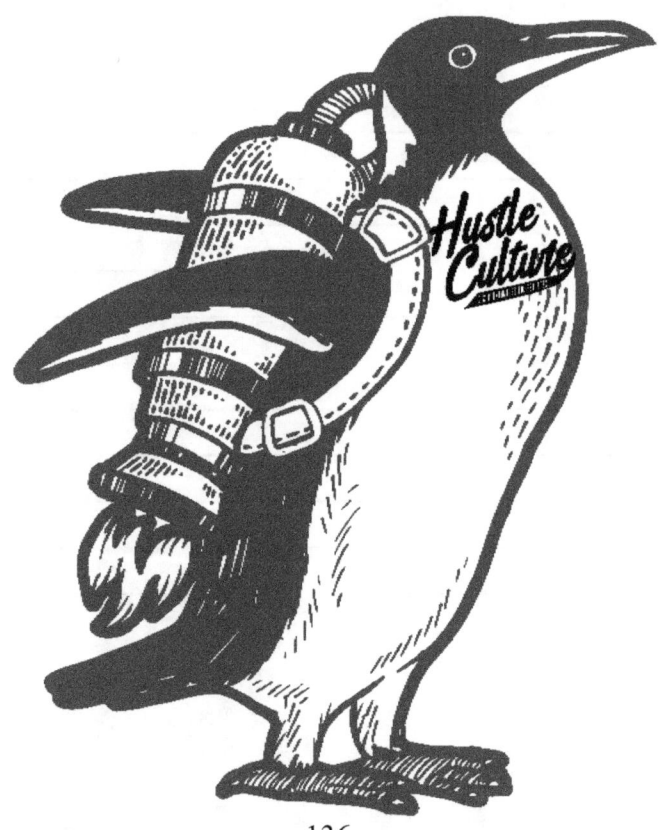

SECTION VI: Hustle Transformation

Okay, Now What?

We started this journey with you at a crossroad. Are you the high school graduate that realizes that college right after high school is not the best option for you? Are you the college graduate that has decided not to go to grad school? Perhaps, you are that corporate executive that plans on leaving your job to start your business. 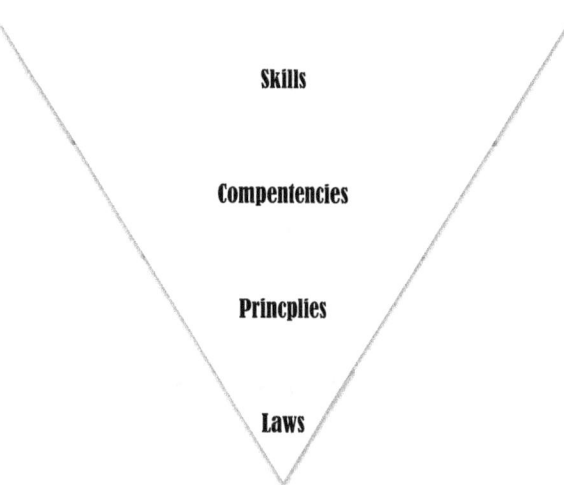 Whatever situation, with this book you are one step closer fulfilling your destiny. Together, we have covered numerous Hustle Culture Skills, Competencies, and Principals but we haven't covered the Hustle Culture Laws. Every skill, Competency, and Principle are linked to three Hustle Culture Laws. These laws are the founding beliefs that makes Hustle Culture, Hustle Culture.

Law One- The Law of Action Planning

Plan for your success. It is essential to coordinate and strategize in order to implement the Skills, Competencies, and Principals outlined in this book.

Set Goals:
- Create a realistic timeline for implementing specific Skills, Competencies, and Principals.
- Have a plan for the monetary investment you will need to implement Skills, Competencies, and Principals.

Investigate and Research the Possibility of Transforming Your Life.
- If you are thinking of changing your career, set-up a meeting with a career coach.
- Take a career assessment test.
- Participate in a professional development center.
- Do research on the need for education or business start-up cost.
- Have a conversation with a person who is in the same business.

Formulate Communication Plans with Stakeholders

- You should have an agreement with other stakeholders such as a spouse or significant other.
- Communicate with your parents or family members about your plans.
- Conduct research on a possible career and or business.
- Put your plan into writing.

In conclusion, make sure you have your plan in writing; this includes your mission, vision, and goals. If you are starting a business, you will need to complete your business plan.

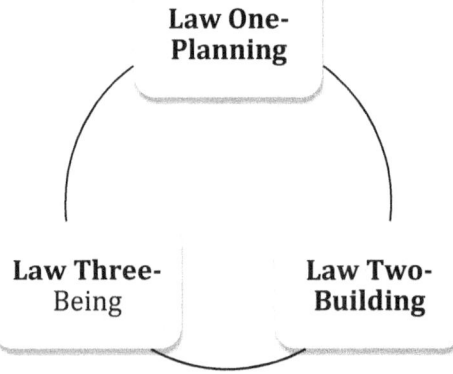

Law Two-Law of Building

Develop a Support System

- Find a mentor
- Start networking both online and locally
- Join associations that are related to the niche of the business or your career interest
- Join online communities that are related to your career or business

Build Based on Your Plan

Building on Skill, Competencies, and Principle:

- Start enhancing the **Skills, Competencies, and Principles** you currently possess.
- If schooling is needed, plan for the educational process.
  - What is the cost of education?
  - If degrees or certificates are a part of that process, how long does it take for you to receive those certificates?
- Regardless of the skillset, take some classes that relate to that field so that you can speak the language.
- Implement everything that we have covered in this book.

Count the Cost

- Do not quit your day job too soon.
- Start a career or business while you are still working.
- Utilize your night and weekends to learn the skills of your new career or business.
- Maintain workforce integrity.
- Learn how to Hustle without added pressure.
- Remember that Hustle Culture is a lifestyle, not an event.
- Be disciplined and consistent.

- Volunteer (Service Related or Non-Profit)
  - If your passion is service-based or a non-profit organization, you may also want to volunteer, just to see if it is the right fit for your vision.

Law Three- Law of Being

Be Willing to Start

You can spend all your time organizing and talking with people about your Hustle; however, your Hustle can only become a reality, if you start! Develop that product, shop that resume, take those courses.

Be Proactive

Align yourself with Hustle and allow for things to happen. This is where you begin to operate your faith. This is where you take control and make things happen. You start to knock on doors, make phone calls. You must always remember that Hustle Culture is about aligning yourself with destiny. This is the time where you can say "I" was born to do this.

Be Dedicated

Hustle Culture is about dedication. The best way to do this is to make a sacrificial investment into your Hustle. That means both time and money. Faith investments in cash towards your vision is the quickest way to activate the process, with a commitment to see things through.

Be realistic

Rome was not built overnight, nor will your Hustle. The Hustle Culture lifestyle will take time; just stay true to the Hustle.

Be Confident

If you do not believe in your Hustle, then no one else will! Confidence is everything.

Be Fearless

Do not allow Fear to make you powerless or ineffective. Do not give in to fear.

Be the Part

Be the person that you inspire to be. Read books written by successful people living their dreams. Let their thoughts become your thoughts;

let their disciplines become your discipline. Eventually, you will begin to see the Hustle come to life.

Be Positive

You will have some good days and some bad days. It is essential that you maintain a positive mindset.

Be Selfish

With Hustle Culture you cannot allow anyone to deter you from your purpose. Cherish your Hustle more than anything else in this world.

Be Willing to Fail

You must remember that you might fail the first time. You may miss the mark the second time. ***But you must be willing to try again!*** You must be ready to dust yourself off and keep moving to fulfill your purpose in life. Failing comes with the Culture, so learn to embrace it and grow because the byproduct of Hustle Culture is a success.

Section VII-Conclusion

Congratulations, you have made it to the end of this very long manual. It has been a journey. We have covered a ton of information, but the process of becoming a Hustle Culture Champion is just beginning. See, the magnificence power of Hustle Culture is people like you!

Your Hustle is forged with a greatness. You and your Hustle are created to impact the lives of others. Your contribution to humanity is so important that it took years to write this book. Years ago, I made it my Hustle to die empty and to leave a legacy of fulfilled dreams for generations to come. It is with that heart, that I wrote this book. Everything in this manual is intended to be your strength in times of weakness and to be your light when you want to give up. Hustle Culture is my walk of faith and hope.

I have always wanted to have my own business in public speaking. However, in my 20's and 30's, I felt the need to have a stable income, to get a paycheck and insurance. I spent years working at being a responsible adult but neglecting my authentic self. Hence, my life was miserable, overworked, and unappreciated. When I decided to live my life based on purpose, things began to change. It was not an overnight process but choosing to be who I felt I was created to be unlocked a Hustle Culture within.

It took years to document my journey! My journey consisted of very humbling situations, horrific circumstances, uncomfortable growth moments and tremendous victories. I know what it means to decide between inauthentic life and Hustle Culture. I know how it feels to need the security of a well-calculated plan for your future. Your purpose and your Hustle never go away. It haunts you until the day that you either die or manifest it.

The issue is that time is not guaranteed. You will never know the outcome of your Hustle if you never go for it! You only get one shot at living life, so you better master the art of living and Hustling it!

The miracle and power of Hustle Culture is in your hands right now! If you are reading this book, fate has connected us. My journey has now become part of your life. Whether you purchased this book from me, ordered the book, received it as a gift, or found the book - it is a part of a plan to help you achieve your purpose and to inspire you on your journey.

If I had chosen a job over my passion, purpose, vision, and mission, then you would not be reading this book. It would be locked away in my mind. This manual would be in my daydreams until I decided to ACT.

I pray that you too decide to ACT and take the path that leads to your greatness. I have faith that as you read this manual, you will never be the same. I am honored that you have read this manual. I am thankful and humbled that I have fulfilled a part of my legacy by sharing these words with you. Now it's up to you to decide to embrace the Hustle Culture and leave your own legacy. Welcome to Hustle Culture!

Section IX-Resources

G & P Unlimited Co.
www.gpunlimitedco.com

Short-Term Goal Tracker

GOAL			GOAL			GOAL		
STRATEGY			STRATEGY			STRATEGY		
MINI GOAL	DATE	REWARD	MINI GOAL	DATE	REWARD	MINI GOAL	DATE	REWARD
GOAL COMPLETE			GOAL COMPLETE			GOAL COMPLETE		
DATE	REWARD		DATE	REWARD		DATE	REWARD	

GOAL			GOAL			GOAL		
STRATEGY			STRATEGY			STRATEGY		
MINI GOAL	DATE	REWARD	MINI GOAL	DATE	REWARD	MINI GOAL	DATE	REWARD
GOAL COMPLETE			GOAL COMPLETE			GOAL COMPLETE		
DATE	REWARD		DATE	REWARD		DATE	REWARD	

G & P Unlimited Co.
www.gpunlimitedco.com

Career Goals Template

PRIMARY CAREER INTEREST	
LONG-TERMS PROFESSIONAL GOALS	
SHORT-TERMS PROFESSIONAL GOALS	
ACTIVITIES TO REACH GOALS	
CURRENT TASKS THAT CONTRIBUTE TO LONG-TERMS GOALS How can these task be emphasized and performed more frequently?	
CURRENT TASKS THAT DO NOT CONTRIBUTE TO LONG-TERMS GOALS How can these task be minimized or eliminated/delegated?	
ADDITIONAL SKILLS/ KNOWLADGE/EXPERIENCE NEEDED TO ATTAIN GOALS	
PROGRESS CHECKPOINT AND TASKS What activities will contribute to reaching goals, and how/when will they be completed and monitored?	

G & P Unlimited Co.
www.gpunlimitedco.com

Goal Brainstorming

1. DEFINE YOUR GOAL
Make your goal SMART – Learn More about this in this month's eBook

2. WHY IS THIS IMPORTANT TO YOU?
This will help you decide how much time and energy is worth investing.

3. WHAT BARRIERS OR OBTACLES ARE THERE?
Identifying and addressing potential bumps sets you up to manage them better when (and if) they arise

4. BREAK IT DOWN INTO STEPS
Break down your goal into a series of smaller steps, this will make it much easier to achieve as you celebrate successes along the way.

5. WHAT SKILLS OR RESOURCES WILL YOU NEED?
Is there something you need to learn or obtain as part of achieving your goal?

6. WHO CAN HELP?
Most things are easier with a buddy. Is there someone who can mentor you or work with you?

G & P Unlimited Co.
www.gpunlimitedco.com

Everything Daily Planner

date: __/__/__

TODAY'S POINT OF FOCUS

TODAY'S SCHEDULE
- 06.00
- 07.00
- 08.00
- 09.00
- 10.00
- 11.00
- 12.00
- 01.00
- 02.00
- 03.00
- 04.00
- 05.00
- 06.00
- 07.00

TO BUY
- ☐
- ☐
- ☐
- ☐
- ☐
- ☐
- ☐
- ☐
- ☐
- ☐

TO DO
- ☐
- ☐
- ☐
- ☐
- ☐
- ☐
- ☐
- ☐
- ☐

make time for:
- o Spiritual Growth
- o Friendship
- o Spontaneous Fun
- o Learning & Study
- o Rest & Relaxation
- o Home Improvement
- o Romance
- o Meditation
- o Exercise
- o Cleaning
- o Creating
- o Nothing

NOTES

BREAKFAST

LUNCH

DINNER

SNACKS

G & P Unlimited Co.
www.gpunlimitedco.com

Weekly To Do

WEEK OF :

MONDAY	TUESDAY	WEDNESDAY	THURSDAY	FRIDAY

SATURDAY	SUNDAY

MUST DO THIS WEEK
- ☐ _____
- ☐ _____
- ☐ _____
- ☐ _____
- ☐ _____
- ☐ _____
- ☐ _____

CALLS TO MAKE
- ☐ _____
- ☐ _____
- ☐ _____
- ☐ _____
- ☐ _____
- ☐ _____
- ☐ _____

EMAILS TO SEND
- ☐ _____
- ☐ _____
- ☐ _____
- ☐ _____
- ☐ _____
- ☐ _____
- ☐ _____

NOTES	TASK				
	☐	☐	☐	☐	☐
	☐	☐	☐	☐	☐

G & P Unlimited Co.
www.gpunlimitedco.com

Weekly Exercise Tracker

	EXERCISE	SET 1		SET 2		SET 3	
SUNDAY	1.	REPS:	WEIGHT:	REPS:	WEIGHT:	REPS:	WEIGHT:
	2.	REPS:	WEIGHT:	REPS:	WEIGHT:	REPS:	WEIGHT:
	3.	REPS:	WEIGHT:	REPS:	WEIGHT:	REPS:	WEIGHT:
	4.	REPS:	WEIGHT:	REPS:	WEIGHT:	REPS:	WEIGHT:
	5.	REPS:	WEIGHT:	REPS:	WEIGHT:	REPS:	WEIGHT:
MONDAY	1.	REPS:	WEIGHT:	REPS:	WEIGHT:	REPS:	WEIGHT:
	2.	REPS:	WEIGHT:	REPS:	WEIGHT:	REPS:	WEIGHT:
	3.	REPS:	WEIGHT:	REPS:	WEIGHT:	REPS:	WEIGHT:
	4.	REPS:	WEIGHT:	REPS:	WEIGHT:	REPS:	WEIGHT:
	5.	REPS:	WEIGHT:	REPS:	WEIGHT:	REPS:	WEIGHT:
TUESDAY	1.	REPS:	WEIGHT:	REPS:	WEIGHT:	REPS:	WEIGHT:
	2.	REPS:	WEIGHT:	REPS:	WEIGHT:	REPS:	WEIGHT:
	3.	REPS:	WEIGHT:	REPS:	WEIGHT:	REPS:	WEIGHT:
	4.	REPS:	WEIGHT:	REPS:	WEIGHT:	REPS:	WEIGHT:
	5.	REPS:	WEIGHT:	REPS:	WEIGHT:	REPS:	WEIGHT:
WEDNESDAY	1.	REPS:	WEIGHT:	REPS:	WEIGHT:	REPS:	WEIGHT:
	2.	REPS:	WEIGHT:	REPS:	WEIGHT:	REPS:	WEIGHT:
	3.	REPS:	WEIGHT:	REPS:	WEIGHT:	REPS:	WEIGHT:
	4.	REPS:	WEIGHT:	REPS:	WEIGHT:	REPS:	WEIGHT:
	5.	REPS:	WEIGHT:	REPS:	WEIGHT:	REPS:	WEIGHT:
THURSDAY	1.	REPS:	WEIGHT:	REPS:	WEIGHT:	REPS:	WEIGHT:
	2.	REPS:	WEIGHT:	REPS:	WEIGHT:	REPS:	WEIGHT:
	3.	REPS:	WEIGHT:	REPS:	WEIGHT:	REPS:	WEIGHT:
	4.	REPS:	WEIGHT:	REPS:	WEIGHT:	REPS:	WEIGHT:
	5.	REPS:	WEIGHT:	REPS:	WEIGHT:	REPS:	WEIGHT:
FRIDAY	1.	REPS:	WEIGHT:	REPS:	WEIGHT:	REPS:	WEIGHT:
	2.	REPS:	WEIGHT:	REPS:	WEIGHT:	REPS:	WEIGHT:
	3.	REPS:	WEIGHT:	REPS:	WEIGHT:	REPS:	WEIGHT:
	4.	REPS:	WEIGHT:	REPS:	WEIGHT:	REPS:	WEIGHT:
	5.	REPS:	WEIGHT:	REPS:	WEIGHT:	REPS:	WEIGHT:
SATURDAY	1.	REPS:	WEIGHT:	REPS:	WEIGHT:	REPS:	WEIGHT:
	2.	REPS:	WEIGHT:	REPS:	WEIGHT:	REPS:	WEIGHT:
	3.	REPS:	WEIGHT:	REPS:	WEIGHT:	REPS:	WEIGHT:
	4.	REPS:	WEIGHT:	REPS:	WEIGHT:	REPS:	WEIGHT:
	5.	REPS:	WEIGHT:	REPS:	WEIGHT:	REPS:	WEIGHT:

G & P Unlimited Co.
www.gpunlimitedco.com

Long Term Goal

WHAT	WHY	REWARD

WHEN

WHEN

ACTION TO TAKE	DUE
	☐
	☐
	☐
	☐
	☐
	☐
	☐
	☐
	☐

REVIEW

WHAT WORKED	WHAT DON'T

Invictus
By Earnest Henley

Out of the night that covers me,
Black as the pit from pole to pole,
I thank whatever gods maybe
For my unconquerable soul.
In the fell clutch of circumstance
I have not winced nor cried aloud.
Under the bludgeonings of chance
My head is bloody, but unbowed.
Beyond this place of wrath and tears
Looms but the Horror of the shade,
And yet the menace of the years
Finds and shall find me unafraid.
It matters not how strait the gate,
How charged with punishments the scroll,
I am the master of my fate,
I am the captain of my soul.

Suggested Reading

Book	Author	Category
The Attention Revolution	Alan Wallace	Stress-management Mediation Personal Development
Business Adventures: Twelve Classic Tales from the World of Wall Street	John Brooks	Business Motivation
The Intelligent Investor	Benjamin Graham	Stocks Personal Finance
Daring Greatly: How the Courage to Be Vulnerable Transforms the Way We Live, Love, Parent, and Lead	Brené Brown	Personal Development
Eat That Frog! 21 Great Ways to Stop Procrastinating and Get More Done in Less Time	Brian Tracy	Personal Development Time Management Organizational
The Meditations of Marcus Aurelius.	Marcus Aurelius.	Personal Development Leadership Wisdom
So Good They Can't Ignore You	Cal Newport	Personal Development Professional Development
Why Didn't They Teach Me This in School?	Cary Siegel	Personal Development Personal Finance
Blue Ocean Strategy: How To Create Uncontested Market Space And Make The Competition Irrelevant	Chan Kim and Renee Mauborgne	Personal Development
Smarter, Faster, Better	Charles Duhigg	Personal Development Time Management Purpose Thinking
The Power of Habit:	Charles Duhigg	Personal Development

Why We Do What We Do in Life and Business		
Virtual Freedom: How to Work with Virtual Staff to Buy More Time, Become More Productive, and Build Your Dream Business	Chris Ducker	Entrepreneurship
An Astronaut's Guide to Life on Earth: What Going to Space Taught Me About Ingenuity, Determination, and Being Prepared for Anything	Chris Hadfield	Personal Development Professional Development
Dream Big	Cristiane Correa	Entrepreneurship
Mindsight	Daniel J. Siegel	Personal Development Mental Health
Thinking, Fast and Slow	Daniel Kahneman	Mental Health Thinking
Getting Things Done: The Art of Stress-Free Productivity	David Allen	Work-Life Balance Personal Development
The Automatic Millionaire	David Bach	Personal Finance
Feeling Good	David D. Burns	Mental Health
The Magic of Thinking Big	David J. Schwartz	Personal Development
The Power of Positive Thinking	Dr. Norman Vincent Peale	Positive Thinking Personal Development
Influence: The Psychology of Persuasion, Revised Edition	Dr. Robert Cialdini	Influence Persuasion Sales
What to Say When You Talk to Your Self	Dr. Shad Helmstetter	Mental Health
The Power of Now	Eckhart Tolle	Emotional Intelligence Personal Development
Why We Do What We Do: Understanding Self-Motivation	Edward L. Deci	Purpose Goals Personal Development

Broke Millennial: Stop Scraping By and Get Your Financial Life Together"	Erin Lowry	Personal Finance Motivational
Crush It! Why NOW Is the Time to Cash In on Your Passion	Gary Vaynerchuk	Entrepreneurship Ecommerce
Talent is Overrated	Geoff Colvin	Purpose Mission Vision Personal Development
10X Rule	Grant Cardone	Organization Time Megaevent
Secrets of the Millionaire Mind	Harv Eker	*Personal Development* *Financial*
The Success Principles	Jack Canfield	Motivation Success
As You Think	James Allen	Thinking Personal Development
Failing Forward	John C. Maxwell	Personal Development
Spark	John Ratey	Fitness Personal Development
The Only Skill That Matters	Jonathan A. Levi	Professional Development
Simplify	Joshua Becker	Minimalization
Philosophy for Life	Jules Evans	Thinking
Love Yourself Like Your Life Depends On	Kamal Ravikant	Personal Development
The Confidence Code: The Science and Art of Self-Assurance	Katty Kay	Personal Development Motivational Confidence
Nice Girls Don't Get the Corner Office: Unconscious Mistakes Women Make That Sabotage Their Careers	Lois P. Frankel	Women Personal Development Success
Outliers The Story of Success	Malcolm Gladwell	Motivational Success Personal Development
Think and Grow Rich-1937	Napoleon Hill.	Thinking Personal Development

Title	Author	Category
The Now Habit: A Strategic Program for Overcoming Procrastination and Enjoying Guilt-Free Play	Neil Fiore	Time Management Organization
Long Walk To Freedom	Nelson Mandela	Motivation
The Last Lecture	Randy Pausch	Motivation
Principles	Ray Dalio	Personal Development
Seagull	Jonathan Livingston	Motivational
What Color Is Your Parachute? 2016: A Practical Manual for Job-Hunters and Career-Changers	Richard N. Bolles	Personal Development Professional Development
The 48 Laws of Power	Robert Greene	Personal Development
Whatcha Gonna Do with That Duck?	Seth Godin	Personal Development
Lean In: Women, Work, and the Will to Lead	Sheryl Sandberg	Women Personal Development Professional Development.
The 7 Habits of Highly Effective People	Stephen. R. Covey	Time Management
The Money Book for the Young, Fabulous & Broke	Suze Orman	Personal Finance
Stop Acting Rich	Thomas Stanley	Personal Finance
The 4-Hour Workweek: Escape 9-5, Live Anywhere, and Join the New Rich	Timothy Ferriss	Ecommerce Personal Development Professional Development
StrengthsFinder 2.0	Tom Rath	Personal Development
Money: Master the Game	Tony Robbins	Personal Finance
Awaken the Giant Within	Tony Robbins	Personal Development
365 Ways to Live Cheap: Your Everyday Guide to Saving Money	Trent Hamm	Personal Finance
Your Money or Your Life	Vicki Robin	Personal Finance
Man's Search For Meaning	Victor. E. Frankl	Purpose Personal Development
Steve Jobs	Walter Isaacson.	Motivational

References

Bibliography

Coleman, K. (2019, August 9). *17 Unwritten Email Etiquette Rules No One Ever Taught You* . Retrieved from BestLife: https://bestlifeonline.com/email-etiquette/

Committee, T. C., Brammer , L., Dumlao, R., Falk, A., Hollander, E., Knutson, E., . . . werner, V. (2011). *Core Competencies in Civic Engagement.* North Andover : Merrimack College.

Conorstone. (n.d.). *Conotstone.* Retrieved from Conorstone: https://www.cornerstoneondemand.com/performance-tips-developing-strong-work-ethic

Cooper, P. (2017, July 13). *New York Fed Highlights Underemployment Among College Graduates.* Retrieved from Forbes: https://www.forbes.com/sites/prestoncooper2/2017/07/13/new-york-fed-highlights-underemployment-among-college-graduates/?sh=5bd04bdc40d8

DeMers, J. (n.d.). *51 Email Etiquette Rules Everyone Should Fllow* . Retrieved from Emial Analytics: https://emailanalytics.com/51-email-etiquette-rules-everyone-should-follow/

Doyle, A. (2020, September 20). *Verbal Communication Skills List and Examples* . Retrieved from The Balance Careers : https://www.thebalancecareers.com/verbal-communication-skills-list-2059698

Doyle, A. (2020, September 26). *What are Sogt Skills* . Retrieved from The Balance Careers : https://www.thebalancecareers.com/what-are-soft-skills-2060852

Erkine, M. B. (2013, December 17). *Saint Leo Blog DEGREE PROGRAMS SAINT LEO LEARNING LIFE BALANCE FINANCIAL AID CAREER ADVICE Why is Work Ethic Important To Career Success.* Retrieved from Saint Leo University : https://www.saintleo.edu/blog/why-developing-a-good-work-ethic-is-essential-to-career-success

Erskine, M. B. (2013, Fevurary 13). *Work Ethic: 5 Easy Steps for Developing a Good Work Ethic.* Retrieved from Saint Leo University : https://www.saintleo.edu/blog/how-to-develop-a-good-work-ethic-in-5-easy-steps

Fitssimmons, W., Lewi, M. M., & Ducey, C. (2006). *Time Out or Burn Out for the Next Generation . Harvard,.* Harvard .

Francisco, M. (2013, Jaunuary 22). *6 Ways to Improve Your Work Ethic, Get Ahead, and Learn the Secrets of Successful Immigrants.* Retrieved from Huffington Post: https://www.huffpost.com/entry/6-ways-to-improve-your-wo_b_2506312

Fullerton. (n.d.). *Telephone Etiquette.* Retrieved from Fullerton Edu: http://www.fullerton.edu/IT/Services/Telecom/FAQ/etiquetteguide.asp

Gallup, S. (2017). *Crisis of Confidence: Current College Students Do Not Feel Prepared for the Workforce.* Strada Gallup.

Gennep, A. v. (1909). *Rites of Passage http://www.brownielocks.com/graduation.html* . Retrieved from http://www.brownielocks.com/graduation.html

Hora, M. T. (2917, Febuary 1). *Beyond The Skill Gap*. Retrieved from National Association of College and Employers: https://www.naceweb.org/career-readiness/trends-and-predictions/beyond-the-skills-gap/

Indeed Editorial Team. (2021, March 8). *10 Common Leadership Styles (Plus How To Find Your Own)* . Retrieved from Indeed : https://www.indeed.com/career-advice/career-development/10-common-leadership-styles

Jennie Hunter. (2003). *Professional Etiquette* . Retrieved from Western Carolina University: http://www.pvamu.edu/pages/1887.asp

Kelly, J. (2019, Nov 14). *Recent College Graduates Have The Highest Unemployment Rate In Decades—Here's Why Universities Are To Blame*. Retrieved from Forbes: https://www.forbes.com/sites/jackkelly/2019/11/14/recent-college-graduates-have-the-highest-unemployment-rate-in-decadesheres-why-universities-are-to-blame/?sh=50484cd3320b

Porteous, C. (2020, November 26). *11 Organizational Skills That Every Smart Leader Needs* . Retrieved from Life Hack : https://www.lifehack.org/818973/organizational-ability

Snyder, K. (2020, March 23). *Omnia*. Retrieved from The 7 Soft Skills You Need to Be Successful: https://www.omniagroup.com/the-7-soft-skills-you-need-to-be-successful/

Taylor, J. (2019). *9 Effective Communication Skills* . Retrieved from Habits For Well Being : https://www.habitsforwellbeing.com/9-effective-communication-skills/

Ward, S. (2008). *8 Rules For Good Customer Service `http://sbinfocanada.about.com/od/customerservice/a/custservrules.htm* . Retrieved from http://sbinfocanada.about.com/od/customerservice/a/custservrules.htm

G & P Unlimited Co.

G & P Unlimited Co is conglomerate of multiple lifestyle Companies and affiliates. We are a multi-industry company and for the past 10 years, we have developed the most exclusive collection of lifestyle brands and services. Our lifestyle brand and service are:

- *G & P Unlimited Co.*
- *Goal Line Coaching*
- *K. A. Perkins*
- *S.N. Perkins*
- *I'ame*
- *Avodah Ministries*
- *Generational Unlimited*
- *Sister Huddle*
- *G & P Quality Homes*
- *Idyllic Parousia*
- *G & P Adventure Co.*
- *Generational Unlimited*
- *Hustle Culture Co.*
- *C.A. Perkins (Affiliate)*
- *Unlimited Innovation*

G & P Unlimited Co. has a strategic advantage as holding conglomerates which include:

- *Savings on media spending*
- *Better accessibility/negotiation*
- *Professional management*
- *Broad range of products and services.*

G & P Unlimited Co. is a close-knit conglomerate who are dedicated to sharing their knowledge and experience though meaningful garments, educational books, inspiring music, and educational courses and more.

G & P Unlimited Co. Mission

G & P Unlimited Co. is Unlimited Lifestyle Company. We promote Hustle mentality and purpose perspective to help you follow your unique path and guide those who are lost or seek assistance. We are always here for people to make sure they live the best life. Our Unlimited Lifestyle brands show that limits exist only in your head.

G& P Unlimited Co. Vision

To be the pioneer of the Unlimited Lifestyle and the leaders in Hustle Culture and Consciousness. To inspire and motivate people to be great in their individual work, worship, and service.

G& P Unlimited Co. Values

Hustle Culture, helping and empowering people are the core values of G & P Unlimited Co. Our success as a company is measured by the success of our customers.

G& P Unlimited Co. Goals

Our Goals at G & P Unlimited Co. are aimed at empowering like-minded people. We offer limitless educational opportunities, books, and music. We inspire to bring Hope and Hustle to the world.

G & P Unlimited Co. Motto

Hope Mentality, a Pursuit Purpose Perspective, and a Hustle Culture. Live Life - Be Unlimited - Become Legendary

G & P Unlimited Co. Tagline

We do it for the Culture! We Hustle for the People!

PoEthics Philosophy

We are committed to being active corporate citizens. Our hallmark work is PoEthics – servant leadership to humanity, outstanding ethical conduct and resolute responsibility to our communities. We believe that service must be entrenched within our ethos, and translated in our Company's culture, to ensure that we are creating an environment that inspires people, both customers and employees, to Live Boldly, to Live Authentically and to Live Unlimited.

Lifestyle Company

Our supporters are activist, artist, blipsters, clergy, civic leaders, educators, entrepreneurs, hipsters, innovators and minimalist who live a life of service to humanity (PoEthics).

Consciousness Culture

We are inspiring supporters to live holistic lives. Our blog and products are centered around helping you to be inspired, motivated, and educated to thrive so when you are in the middle of the Hustle you are performing at your peak.

GNR8N Unlimited

Generation Unlimited Organization was formed to help eradicate the barriers that disadvantaged youth and young adult's encounter. At G & P, we know that while providing information and inspiring books are helpful, it must be coupled with action. For this reason, your continual support of G & P Unlimited Company and Brands will help us provide free services such as shelter, food, counseling, educational resources, social service resources, job readiness resources, and etc.,

http://generationunlimited.com

When You Support Our Company

When you support or make purchases of products and services from G & P Unlimited Co., you are helping us help people. Through your generous support, we can make the online version of books like TIKVAH for free. G & P Unlimited Co. also donates 10% of company profits to our Generation Unlimited Organization.

Attention Vendors

Any person, business, organization, or group can become a distributor of G & P Unlimited products. By simply purchasing a minimum number of 10 books you are entitled to G & P Unlimited Co. the wholesale rate. The discount for our products varies according to the specific product.

To continue to receive ongoing wholesale rates, you must apply and at least purchase $200 worth of G&P Products per quarter.

Distribution Membership Benefits
- *Newsletters*
- *Economic Opportunities*
- *Sample Products*
- *Promotional Pre-Released Books (PDF)*
- *Networking Events*
- *Entrepreneurial Opportunities*

Distribution Membership Requirements
- *Application on File*
- *Purchase at least $200.00 worth of products per quarter (3 months period).*

For more information visit us at www.gpunlimitedco.com or email us at info@gpunltd.com

Become a Facilitator

If you have been changed by our books become an G & P Unlimited Co. Facilitator. This is a two-day intensive program designed to provide you with the skills you need to create powerful and transformative workshops. G & P Unlimited Co. Facilitator training will provide you with the tools you need to enhance your confidence and create new depth to your presentations.

You will learn how to:

- *Create and engaging environment that stimulate discussion.*
- *Lead session that that will leave your participants feeling touched, open, valued, and nurtured.*
- *Generate an environment where women and men communicate more authentically.*
- *Listen profoundly*
- *Create a powerful ability to relate with strangers quickly and easily.*
- *Be more open to others and able to give and receive comfortably.*
- *Create strong boundaries for yourself without shutting others down.*

You will also learn:

* *The skills that can be used to sell each of the products while also creating your own stream of income.*
* *How to use the **Advertisement Tool Kit** to Generate Sales or Host Coach Talk Parties*
* *How to set-up a **Successful Influencer and Affiliate** income using our products.*
* *Much More*

For more information about this wonderful opportunity, don't hesitate to contact info@gpunltd.com or visit us online at www.gpunlimitedco.com

About the Author

Highly dedicated, innovative, and goal-driven, K. A. Perkins is a maverick Author, Educator, Consultant, and Influencer whose underlying mission is to deeply empower others to unlock their full potential. As the CEO of G & P Unlimited Co and holding a strong track record of instilling positive self-development transformations, K. A. enjoys every moment of utilizing his creative-eye, past experiences, and rooted passion for guiding others towards becoming the best versions of themselves.

Growing up with humble beginnings, K. A. learned early on the true meaning behind commitment, resilience, and a strong work ethic. These core principles, along with intense perseverance, are what shaped him to overcome disappointments and hardships in life and achieve monumental success. After reaching this balancing point, K. A. chose to fulfill a promise he had made to his younger self, a promise to share the tough lessons he faces during his journey in hopes that valuable information will become the stepping stones for others to learn from and thrive. Not only has K. A. done just that by launching his brand with a fashionable twist, but he is also a loving father and husband who is dedicated to setting a prime example of how a real man is supposed to be through his efforts.

In the end, nothing makes K. A. happier than being able to help others unlock the quality of life and confidence they deserve and influencing a future generation composed of true world changers.

Whether it be via fashion, news, information, events, and media, K. A. has a true ardency for what he does and demonstrated that by developing G & P Unlimited Co on a foundation of authenticity, integrity, and trust and raising the urban streetwear fashion bar. This, in conjunction with his keen artistic nature and reputation promoting self-development that society as a whole can benefit from.

A proud HBCU graduate and member of Alpha Phi Alpha Fraternity Incorporated, K.A. Perkins can give you the solidifying confidence that you have come to the right place to advance your life and style to new prospering levels.

INVITE K.A. PERKINS TO SPEAK TO YOUR NEXT EVENT

If you would like for K.A. Perkins or a member of the G & P Unlimited Team to come speak, please contact us at info@gpunltd.com.

Current Books
- Tikvah

Upcoming Books

- Pearls of Possibility
- The Shift

For More Products and Updates Visit https://gpunltd.com or https://kaperkins.com

G & P Unlimited Co.

Hope Mentality, a Pursue Perspective, and a Hustle Culture. -Live Life-Be Unlimited-Become Legendary

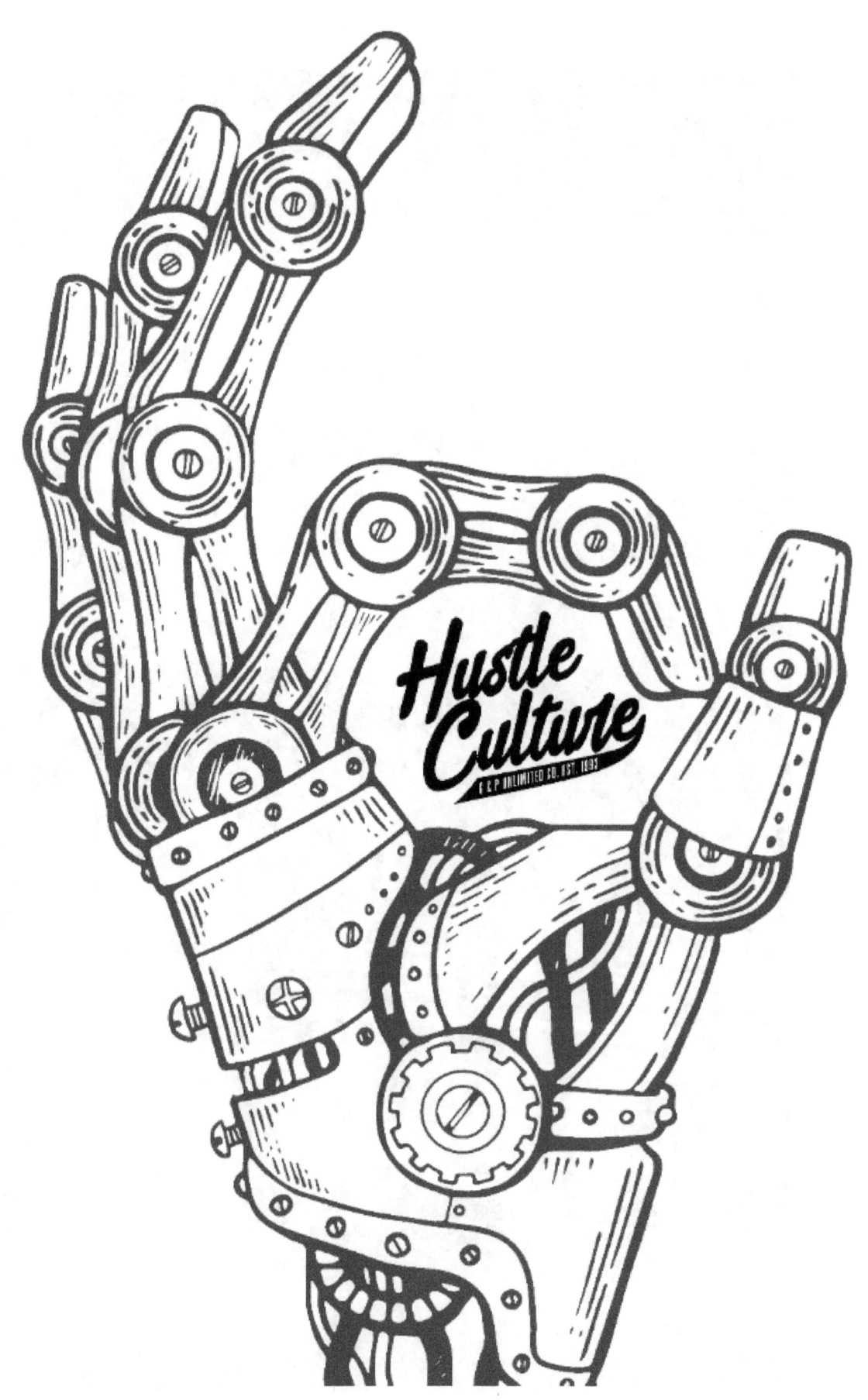

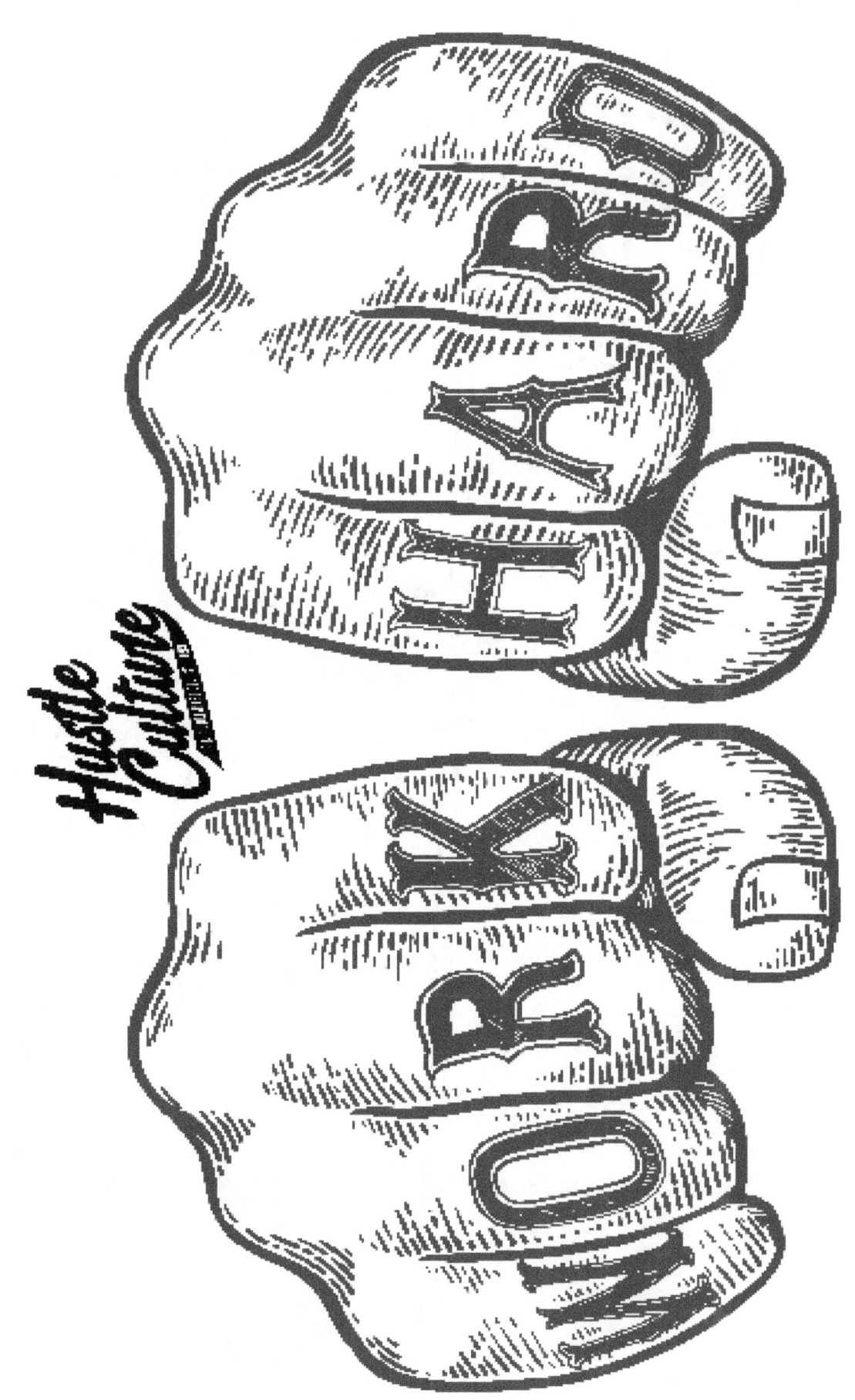

www.ingramcontent.com/pod-product-compliance
Lightning Source LLC
Chambersburg PA
CBHW080735230426
43665CB00020B/2748